I0065388

99 Financial Terms

Every Beginner, Entrepreneur & Business Should Know

Financial IQ Series #1

Published March 26, 2019

Revision 2.3

financial-dictionary.info

Applicable law may not allow the limitation or exclusion of liability or incidental or consequential damages, so the above limitation or exclusion may not apply to you. In no event shall the Author's total liability to you for all damages, losses, and causes of action (whether in contract, tort, including but not limited to, negligence or otherwise) exceed the amount paid by you, if any, for this book.

Facts and information are believed to be accurate at the time they were placed in this book. All data provided in this book is to be used for information purposes only. The information contained within is not intended to provide specific legal, financial or tax advice, or any other advice whatsoever, for any individual or company and should not be relied upon in that regard. The services described are only offered in jurisdictions where they may be legally offered. Information provided is not all-inclusive and is limited to information that is made available and such information should not be relied upon as all-inclusive or accurate.

You are advised to do your own due diligence when it comes to making business decisions and should use caution and seek the advice of qualified professionals. You should check with your accountant, lawyer, or professional advisor, before acting on this or any information. You may not consider any examples, documents, or other content in this eBook or otherwise provided by the Author to be the equivalent of professional advice.

The Author assumes no responsibility for any losses or damages resulting from your use of any link, information, or opportunity contained in this book or within any other information disclosed by the author in any form whatsoever.

About the Author

Thomas Herold is a successful entrepreneur, mediator, author, and personal development coach. He published over 35 books with over 200,000 copies distributed worldwide and the founder of seven online businesses.

For over ten years Thomas Herold has studied the monetary system and has experienced some profound insights on how money and wealth are related. After three years of successful investing in silver, he released 'Building Wealth with Silver - How to Profit From The Biggest Wealth Transfer in History' in 2012. One of the first books that illustrate in a remarkable, simple way the monetary system and its consequences.

He is the founder and CEO of the 'Financial Terms Dictionary' book series and website, which explains in detail and comprehensive form over 1000 financial terms. In his financial book series, he informs in detail and with practical examples all aspects of the financial sector. His educational materials are designed to help people get started with financial education.

In his 2018 released book 'The Money Deception', Mr. Herold provides the most sophisticated insight and shocking details about the current monetary system. Never before has the massive manipulation of money caused so much economic inequality in the world. In spite of these frightening facts, 'The Money Deception' also provides remarkable and simple solutions to create abundance for all people, and it's a must read if you want to survive the global monetary transformation that's underway right now.

In 2019 he released an entirely new financial book series explaining in detail and with practical examples over 1000 financial terms. The 'Herold Financial IQ Series' contains currently of 16 titles covering every category of the financial market.

Please leave your review on Amazon

This book and the Financial IQ Series is self-published and the author does not have a contract with one of the five largest publishers, which are able to support the author's work with advertising. If you like this book, please consider leaving a solid 5-star review on Amazon.

https://www.amazon.com/author/thomasherold

Herold Financial IQ Series

There are 16 books in this financial terms series available. Please see an overview and available formats on Amazon.

Financial IQ Series on Amazon

Introduction

Whenever you hear someone speak personal finance, do you feel like you're learning a foreign language? Do you feel lost when reading or hearing financial terminology from your bank, insurance, investment agent or the IRS?

You're not alone!

For instance, feeling confident when discussing the business's financial needs should be a priority for every small business owner. After all, you represent the heart and soul of your business in the marketplace. Knowing the "language" of business finance is an integral part of your job as the owner.

The good news is that you don't have to be an accountant or a financial planner to negotiate in the world of business finance. This practical glossary contains 99 important, and most commonly used business finance terms and definitions in alphabetical order. It was written with an emphasis to quickly grasp the context without using jargon.

Every financial term is explained in detail, with clear and concise article style description and practical examples.

Now, whether you are a salaried person, a startup enthusiast, a business owner or a common man, these set of 99 financial basics shall help you manage your money in a much better way.

Make Financial Terms Less of a Mystery

In order to become savvy about your own finances, you need to understand a few useful financial definitions. This compilation of financial terms is a comprehensive list of various financial words or concepts that you are likely to come across in your financial expedition.

Table Of Contents

Adjustable Rate Mortgage (ARM)

Adjustable Rate Mortgages, also known by their acronym ARM's, are those mortgages whose interest rates change from time to time. These changes commonly occur based on an index. As a result of changing interest rates, payments will rise and fall along with them.

Adjustable Rate Mortgages involve a number of different elements. These include margins, indexes, discounts, negative amortization, caps on payments and rates, recalculating of your loan, and payment options. When considering an adjustable rate mortgage, you should always understand both the most that your monthly payments might go up, as well as your ability to make these higher payments in the future.

Initial payments and rates are important to understand with these ARM's. They stay in effect for only certain time frames that run from merely a month to as long as five years or longer. With some of these ARM's, these initial payments and rates will vary tremendously from those that are in effect later in the life of the loan. Your payments and rates can change significantly even when interest rates remain level. A way to determine how much this will vary on a particular ARM loan is to compare the annual percentage rate and the initial rate. Should this APR prove to be much greater than the initial rate, then likely the payments and rates will similarly turn out to be significantly greater when the loan adjusts.

It is important to understand that the majority of Adjustable Rate Mortgages' monthly payments and interest rates will vary by the month, the quarter, the year, the three year period, and the five year time frame. The time between these changes in rate is referred to as the adjustment period. Loans that feature one year periods are called one year ARM's, as an example.

These Adjustable Rate Mortgages' interest rates are comprised of two portions of index and margin. The index actually follows interest rates themselves. Your payments are impacted by limits on how far the rate can rise or fall. As the index rises, so will your interest rates and payments generally. As the index declines, your monthly payments could similarly fall, assuming that your ARM is one that adjusts down. ARM rates can be based on a number of different indexes, including LIBOR the London Interbank Offered rate, COFI the Cost of Funds Index, and a CMT one year constant maturity Treasury security. Other lenders use their own proprietary model.

Margin proves to be the premium to the rate that a lender itself adds. This is commonly a couple of percentage points that are added directly to the index rate amount. These amounts vary from one lender to the next, and are commonly fixed during the loan term. The fully indexed rate is comprised of index plus margin. When the loan's initial rate turns out to be lower than the fully indexed rate, this is referred to as a discounted index rate. So an index that sat at five percent and had a three percent margin tacked on would be a fully indexed rate of eight percent.

Affidavit

An Affidavit is a declaration in writing which includes a sworn oath or positive confirmation that written contents are factual and true. These declarations and statements could be made related to court cases. They also could be made to support an important document as with mortgage applications or tax returns.

Though many people may not be aware of it, a great number of forms prove to be affidavits. This is because they have a line that states the individuals have filled in the form to the best of their knowledge. The line must also mention that deliberately entering information that is incorrect will lead to perjury charges. If a person is found guilty of perjury charges, it can lead to significant time spent in jail.

The word affidavit is originally taken from the Latin. The Latin roots signifies that individuals have pledged their faith with complete knowledge of the law. It is interesting that affidavits are always voluntarily undertaken documents. This means that no parties in a court case are able to make a person give such statement under oath. Courts can force individuals to give deposition accounts. Depositions differ from an affidavit. They may both be statements that are written, but depositions will be cross examined in a court.

Affidavits must involve knowledge that is personally known by the individual who declares them. This means that persons who do not include information of which they were unaware will not be punished or deemed to be in perjury. Personal knowledge can cover a person's opinion too. In such cases, the statement must be unequivocally stated to be opinion instead of a known fact. Any individual is allowed to provide an affidavit if he or she maintains the necessary mental ability to comprehend how serious the oath given actually is. This is why guardians of mentally ill patients are able to provide such an affidavit on their behalf.

These documents are generally formally witnessed by a qualified official such as a notary public or an account clerk. Notaries are agents who receive a small fee in exchange for witnessing the signing of legal documents for individuals, as with mortgage forms or real estate transactions. This witness signing the document means that the person pledges that the information is accurate and realizes how important this oath is. Documents like these can be utilized in court as evidence. They can also be submitted alongside supporting materials with various kinds of transactions, including for social services.

Individuals who sign affidavits should be extremely careful that they read the documents several times, especially if another individual is recording them. This is because the documents are oaths which are legally binding. The statements contained within must be correctly and clearly related. When the signor recognizes errors in the document, as with facts on a mortgage application, these need to be corrected in advance of signing. This is more important than the inconvenience it will cause the officials who have written down the information and who are witnessing the signing and oath that accompanies it.

Annual Percentage Rate (APR)

The annual percentage rate, or APR, is the actual interest rate that a loan charges each year. This single percentage number is truthfully used to represent the literal annual expense of using money over the life span of a given loan. Annual percentage rate not only covers interest charged, but can also be comprised of extra costs or fees that are attached to a given loan transaction.

Credit cards and loans commonly offer differing explanations for transaction fees, the structure of their interest rates, and any late fees that are assessed. The annual percentage rate provides an easy to understand formula for expressing to borrowers the real and actual percentage number of fees and interest so that they can measure these up against the rates that other possible lenders will charge them.

Annual percentage rate can include many different elements besides interest. With a nominal APR, it simply involves the rate of a given payment period multiplied out to the exact numbers of payment periods existing in a year. The effective APR is often referred to as the mathematically true rate of interest for a given year. Effective APR's are commonly the fees charged plus the rate of compound interest.

On a home mortgage, effective annual percentage rates could factor in Private Mortgage Insurance, discount points, and even processing costs. Some hidden fees do not make their ways into an effective APR number. Because of this, you should always read the fine print surrounding an APR and the costs associated with a mortgage or loan. As an example of how an effective APR can be deceptive with mortgages, the one time fees that are charged in the front of a mortgage are commonly assumed to be divided over a loan's long repayment period. If you only utilize the loan for a short time frame, then the APR number will be thrown off by this. An effective APR on a mortgage might look lower than it actually is when the loan will be paid off significantly earlier than the term of the loan.

The government created the concept of annual percentage rate to stop loan companies and credit cards issuers from deceiving consumers with fancy expressions of interest charges and fees. The law requires that all loan issuers and credit card companies have to demonstrate this annual percentage rate to all customers. This is so the consumers will obtain a fair comprehension of the true rates that are associated with their particular transactions. While credit card companies are in fact permitted to promote their monthly basis of interest rates, they still have to clearly show the actual annual percentage rate to their customers in advance of a contract or agreement being signed by the consumer.

Annual percentage rate is sometimes confused with annual percentage yield. This can be vastly different from the APR. Annual percentage yield includes calculations of compounded interest in its numbers.

Appraisal

Appraisals are professionally done estimates of a property's real value. These are conducted by appraisers. Many things can have an appraisal done on them, including smaller items like artwork or jewelry, as well as larger things like businesses, commercial buildings, or homes.

Appraisals are commonly required before many different transactions can be performed. In advance of getting a house, piece of jewelry, or an artwork insured, appraisals must be performed. Homes and offices have to be appraised for insurance, loans, and tax purposes. Appraisals ensure that these loans and insurance policies are comparable to the property's tangible market value.

Several different types of appraisals can be performed. Real property appraisal involves properly estimating Real Estate value. Personal property appraisal involves determining the worth of valuable individual objects like expensive china, jewelry, pottery, artwork, heirlooms, and antiques. Mass appraisals merge real property and personal property appraisals into a single appraisal. Business value appraisals consider all of the valuable tangible and intangible assets that a business owns, including logos, services, equipment, property, inventory, other assets and goodwill.

Perhaps the most commonly used type of appraisal is a home appraisal. Home appraisals prove to be professionally done surveys of a house to come up with an opinion or estimate of the home's value on the market. These kinds of appraisals are usually performed for banks that are considering the approval of a loan for a person purchasing a home. Such home appraisals turn out to be detailed reports. These cover many things including the home's neighborhood, the house's condition, how rapidly area houses sell, and what comparable houses actually sell for at the time.

Such a home appraisal could similarly be done for a replacement value for insurance purposes or as a sales comparison in marketing a home, as well. Cost and replacement appraisals determine what the actual cost to completely replace your home would be if something destroyed the house. This type of appraisal is most often employed for new houses. Sales comparison appraisals more often examine various additional properties within your house's neighborhood to determine at what price they are presently selling. The appraiser will then determine how such houses compare and contrast against your particular home.

Home appraisals commonly cost in the range of from $300 to $500 when people decide to order one done themselves. Such appraisals are not often accepted by banks. They will want to have their own contracted appraiser make the estimate in order to get a more independent number that they trust.

Home appraisers are always licensed by the state in which they operate. The highest of ethical standards are demanded of them. Their sole purpose is to act as an independent third party who will give their truthful opinion of a home's market value. Appraisers are not supposed to be associated with any party that is involved in the selling of a home.

Assets

Assets are any thing that can be owned by a company or an individual person. These are able to be sold for cash. Commonly, assets produce income or give value to the owner.

In the world of financial accounting, assets prove to be economic resources. They can be physical objects or intangible concepts that can be utilized and owned to create value. Assets are deemed to have real and positive value for their owners. Assets must also be convertible into cash, which itself is furthermore considered to be an asset.

There are several different types of assets as measured by accountants and accounting processes. These might be current assets, longer term assets, intangible assets, or deferred assets. Current assets include cash and other items that are readily and easily able to be sold to raise cash. Longer term assets are those that are held and useful for great periods of time, including such physical items as factory plants, real estate, and equipment. Intangible assets are non physical rights or concepts, like patents, trademarks, goodwill, and copyrights. Finally, deferred assets are those that involve monies spent now for the costs in the future of things like rent, insurance, or interest.

Though tangible, physical assets are not hard to conceptualize, intangible assets are often confusing for people to understand. Even though these are not physical items that may be touched, they still have value that can be controlled and sold to raise cash. Intangible assets include rights and resources which provide a company with a form of marketplace advantage. These can cover many different elements beyond those listed above, such as computer programs, stocks, bonds, and even accounts receivable.

On balance sheets, tangible assets are commonly divided into further categories. These include fixed assets and current assets. Fixed assets are objects that are immobile or not easily transported, such as buildings, office locations, and equipment. Current assets are comprised of inventory that a business holds. Balance sheets of companies keep track of a firm's assets and their value as expressed in monetary terms. These assets are both the cash and other items that the business or person owns.

Assets should never be confused with liabilities. Assets create positive cash flow that represents value or money coming into a business, organization, or individual's accounts. Liabilities are obligations that have to be paid and that create negative cash flow, or take money out of a business, individual, or organization's accounts. As an example of the difference between the two, assets would be houses that are rented out that bring in more rent every month than the expenses, interest, and upkeep of the houses. Liabilities would be homes that have payments that must be paid every month and do not provide any income stream to effectively offset this.

Bankruptcy

Bankruptcy is a term that refers to the elimination or restructuring of a person or company's debt. Three principal different types of bankruptcy filing are available. These are the personal bankruptcy options of Chapter 7 and Chapter 13 filings, and the business bankruptcy restructuring option of Chapter 11.

Individuals avail themselves of Chapter 7 or Chapter 13 bankruptcy filings when their financial situations warrant significant help. With a Chapter 7 filing, all of an individual's debt is erased through discharge. This provides a new start for the debtor. Due to changes in laws made back in October 2005, not every person is able to obtain this type of total debt relief any longer. As a result of this new bankruptcy law, a means test came into being that prospective bankruptcy filers must successfully pass if they are to prove eligibility for this kind of bankruptcy relief.

The net effect of this new test is that consumers find it much more difficult to qualify for total debt elimination under Chapter 7. Besides the means test, the cost of bankruptcy attorneys has now risen dramatically by upwards of a hundred percent as a result of the new laws. Before these laws went into effect, Chapter 7 filings represented around seventy percent of all personal filings for bankruptcy. Chapter 7 offered the individual the advantage of simply walking away from debts that they might be capable of paying back with sufficient time and some interest rate help.

Chapter 13 Bankruptcy filings prove to be much like debt restructuring procedures. In these proceedings, a person's creditors are made to agree to the repayment of principal and zero interest on debts over a longer span of time. The individual gets to keep all of her or his assets in this form of filing. The most common motivation for Chapter 13 proves to be a desire to stop a foreclosure on a home. Individuals are able to achieve this by halting foreclosure proceedings and catch up on back mortgage payments. Once a court examines the debtor's budget, it will sign off on the plan for repayment proposed by the person. Depending on the level of an individual's income, he or she may have no choice but to file a Chapter 13 filling, as a result to the 2005 law changes.

Companies and corporations that are in financial distress may avail themselves of bankruptcy protection as well. Chapter 11 allows for such businesses to have protection from their creditors while they restructure their debt. Some individuals who have a higher income level will take advantage of this form of filing as well, since it does not place income restrictions on the entity filing. It has been instrumental in saving many large and well known companies over the years, including K-Mart, that actually emerged strong enough from the Chapter 11 bankruptcy to buy out higher end rival Sears afterward.

Bitcoin Currency (BTC)

Bitcoin is the name of a new electronic currency. An unknown individual who called himself Satoshi Nakamoto created this currency in 2009. This world's first widespread virtual currency appeals to many individuals because there are no banks or governments involved in issuing, trading, spending, or processing the transactions. There are also no transaction fees involved. Owners do not have to provide their actual identity to use them.

Bitcoin users like that they are able to purchase goods and services completely anonymously. They also enjoy the inexpensive and simple to use international payment system. This exists because this currency is not heavily regulated nor tied to any single bank or nation. Small businesses tend to like Bitcoin since they do not have to pay any credit card usage fees.

Many speculators have purchased Bitcoins for investment. Booms and busts in this currency are all too common. Those who bought in to the crypto currency early made spectacular returns as the value skyrocketed with growing demand. Others lost fortunes as the price of the Bitcoins subsequently crashed in value.

There are several ways to obtain these Bitcoins. Users buy them on open marketplaces known as Bitcoin exchanges. Those who wish to have them can buy and sell it with a variety of different currencies. Mt. Gox was the largest Bitcoin marketplace until it spectacularly collapsed and went bankrupt. Many clients who held their Bitcoins at Mt. Gox lost most of their money there at the time.

Individuals also buy and sell Bitcoins by transferring them to each other and by paying with them. They can do this with their computers or mobile apps. This is much like sending cash with a digital service like PayPal.

A last way to obtain Bitcoins is by mining them. Mining is the way that individuals create new Bitcoins. They do this by utilizing computers to solve complicated math problems or puzzles. When such a puzzle is solved, 25 Bitcoins are awarded to the group which solves them.

Owners keep their Bitcoins in a digital wallet. This can be stored on a personal computer or in the cloud. A virtual wallet is much like an electronic bank account which permits owners to receive or send Bitcoins, to save their money, or to pay for their goods and services. These wallets do not receive the protection of FDIC insurance as do traditional bank accounts.

To users, Bitcoins are simply computer programs or mobile apps which give the owners the Bitcoin wallet. The payment system is easier to utilize than is a credit card or debit card purchase. An individual does not require a merchant account in order to receive the currency. All an individual has to do to make a payment is to put the payment amount and address of the recipient then click send.

An important fact about Bitcoin is that no one owns the actual network. Bitcoin users control the Bitcoin currency. Various developers work on the software to improve it. Users are able to decide which version or software they use it on, which prohibits developers from forcefully changing the operation. For the software to work properly, all Bitcoin users have to work with programs that abide by the same rules.

As with most new currencies Bitcoin is not without problems. When digital wallets are left in the cloud, some servers have been hacked and coins stolen. Bitcoin exchanges like Mt. Gox have failed. Other companies have disappeared with their clients' Bitcoins. When the wallets stay on a person's computer, they can be destroyed by viruses or accidentally deleted.

Increasing government regulation appears to be in the future of Bitcoin and other crypto currencies. Because of the anonymous nature of the currency, they have evolved into the preferred payment method for illegal activities such as drugs and smuggling. Governments are concerned about being able to trace these types of activities back to the users. They are also worried about not being able to tax transactions made in Bitcoin currency.

Blockchain

Blockchain refers to a technology that serves as a means of structuring and storing data. As such it is the ultimate foundation of the revolutionary crypto-currencies such as Bitcoin and Ether. The true breakthrough in coding capability permits participants to share digital ledgers back and forth over a computer network. Its genius and appeal lies in the fact that it does not require a central authority to run or oversee it. Since there is no meddling central authority like a central bank or boss to the system, no one party can interfere with the financial records.

In other words, the straight math makes sure that all the parties who participate are honest with each other. Blockchain is made up of concatenated transactions blocks. Nowadays, the technology has become so important and offers so many future possibilities for real world applications that over forty of the world's biggest and most important financial firms are experimenting with uses for it.

Blockchains are also public record ledgers of all transactions in a crypto-currency which have ever taken place. For this reason, the chain is always expanding as every new record adds additional completed blocks to it. These become a part of the blockchain via a chronological and linear fashioned order. Every participating node receives a copy of this blockchain as it is updated. Nodes are computers which share a Bitcoin network connection that utilizes the system to validate and relay such transactions which were performed in it. The chain comes as an auto download once a computer network joins up to the Bitcoin network. This chain maintains full information on all balances and appropriate addresses from the very first transaction ever all the way to the latest one which has been performed utilizing the block.

In the end, it is this blockchain that represents the primary technological advance offered by Bitcoin. It amounts to the proof and record of every transaction performed using the network. The blocks represent the current record in the chain that will ultimately record all or at least some of the recent transaction. After it is finished, this block will join the chain as part and parcel of the current and permanent database. Once a block is spoken for, a new block will become generated. Myriads of such blocks exist in the chain. They are linked one to another, much like a physical chain, in their correct chronological and linear order. Each block contains the hash of the prior block in it.

It is always helpful to consider a real world example to better understand a somewhat complex concept like this one. Traditional banking is a solid analogy. This blockchain is much like a complete history of banking records and transactions. Bitcoin transactions must be chronologically entered in the blockchain as real world banking transactions are at financial institutions. Such blocks are something like the statements recording individual bank accounts and banking transactions.

The protocol of Bitcoin is based upon all nodes in the system sharing the blockchain's database. A complete and unaltered copy of the chain will include records of all the transactions in Bitcoin which have ever been executed. This delivers useful insights into the quantity of value that a specific address owned at any time in the past.

The problem with the ever growing nature of the chain is that it has become so very large with over a decade of increasing size that synchronization and storage have become serious issues. These days, the average time of a new block appearing on the chain amounts to only ten minutes. Mining, the process of unlocking new BTC, is adding the majority of new blocks to the chain these days.

Bonds

Bonds are also known as debt instruments, fixed income securities, and credit securities. A bond is actually an IOU contract where the terms of the bond, interest rate, and date of repayment are all particularly defined in a legal document. If you buy a bond at original issue, then you are literally loaning the issuer money that will be repaid to you at a certain time, along with periodic interest payments.

Bonds are all classified under one of three categories in the United States. The first of these are the highest rated, safest category of Federal Government debt and its associated agencies. Treasury bills and treasury bonds fall under this first category. The second types of bonds are bonds deemed to be safe that are issued by companies, states, and cities. These first two categories of bonds are referred to as investment grade. The third category of bonds involves riskier types of bonds that are offered by companies, states, and cities. Such below investment grade bonds are commonly referred to as simply junk bonds.

Bonds' values rise and fall in directly opposite correlation to the movement of interest rates. As interest rates fall, bonds rise. When interest rates are rising, bonds prices fall. These swings up and down in interest rates and bond prices are not important to you if you buy a bond and hold it until the pay back, or maturity, date. If you choose to sell a bond before maturity, the price that it realizes will be mostly dependent on what the interest rates prove to be like at the time.

Bonds' investment statuses are rated by the credit rating agencies. These are Standard & Poor's, Moody's, and Fitch Ratings. All bond debt issues are awarded easy to understand grades, such as A+ or B. In the last few years of the financial crisis, these credit rating agencies were reprimanded for having awarded some companies bonds' too high grades considering the risks that the companies undertook. This was especially the case with the bonds of banks, investment companies, and some insurance outfits.

Understanding the bond markets is a function of comprehending the yield curves. Yield curves turn out to be pictorial representations of a bond's interest rate and the date that it reaches maturity, rendered on a graph.

Learning to understand and read these curves, and to figure out the spread between such curves, will allow you to make educated comparisons between various issues of bonds.

Some bonds are tax free. These are those bonds that are offered by states and cities. Such municipal bonds, also known as munis, help to raise funds that are utilized to pay for roads, schools, dams, and various other projects. Interest payments made on these municipal bonds are not subject to Federal taxes. This makes them attractive to some investors.

Brokers

Brokers are professional intermediaries that work on behalf of both a seller and a buyer. When brokers function as agents on behalf of only a buyer or seller, they become representatives and principal parties in any deal. Brokers should not be confused with agents, who instead work on the behalf of a single principal. In the financial world, there are stock brokers, commodity brokers, and option brokers.

Stock brokers are highly regulated broker professionals that sell and buy stock shares and related securities. They work on the part of investors who purchase and sell such securities. Stock brokers transact through either Agency Only Firms or market makers in a given security. These types of brokers are commonly employees of brokerage firms, such as Morgan Stanley, Prudential, or UBS.

Stock brokers are essential in stock transactions, since these exchanges of stocks can only occur between two individuals who are actual members of the exchange in question. A regular investor can not simply enter a stock exchange like the NASDAQ and ask to buy or sell a stock. This is the role that brokers fulfill.

Within the stock broker realm, three different kinds of broker services exist. One of these is advisory dealing, in which a broker makes recommendations to the client of what types of shares to purchase and sell, yet allows the investor to enact the ultimate decision. A second type is an execution only broker, who will simply transact the customer's specific buying and selling instructions. Finally, discretionary dealing involves brokers who learn all about the customer's goals in investing then carry out trades for the customer based on his or her interests.

These same functions are carried out by other financial market brokers as well. Commodities brokers deal in commodities contracts for clients in commodities such as gold, silver, wheat, and oil. Commodities contracts are comprised of options, futures, and financial derivatives. These commodities brokers act as middle men to an investor to transact buy and sell orders on such commodities exchanges as the New York Mercantile Exchange, Commodities Mercantile Exchange, and New York Board of

Trade.

Options brokers deal in options on stocks, commodities, or currencies, depending on what their area of specialty proves to be. They specialize in providing research, trading, and education on options to individual investor clients. Besides handling the main options that include straddles, option spreads, and covered calls, a number of options brokers facilitate trade in related fields that include ETF's, stocks, bonds, and mutual funds.

Brokers in the financial world are typically regulated by one oversight group or another. Stock brokers, for example, are licensed and overseen by the Securities Exchange Commission. They must pass an exam called the Series 7 in order to practice their trade as a stock broker. Commodities brokers, on the other hand, must obtain a Series 3 license from the Financial Industry Regulatory Authority. They are closely monitored by the Commodities Futures Trading Commission. Options brokers are monitored by the regulatory agency associated with the area of options that they trade.

Capital Gains

Capital gains refer to profits that arise when you sell a capital asset like real estate, stocks, and bonds. These proceeds must be above the purchase price to qualify as capital gains. A capital gain is also the resulting difference between a low buying price and a high selling price that leads to a financial gain for investors. The opposite of capital gains are capital losses, which result from selling such a capital asset at a price lower than for what you purchased it. Capital gains can pertain to investment income that is associated with tangible assets like financial investments of bonds and stocks and real estate. They may also result from the sale of intangible assets that include goodwill.

Capital gains are also one of the two principal types of investor income. The other is passive income. With capital gains' forms of income, large, one time amounts are realized on an asset or investment. There is no chance for the income to be continuous or periodic, as with passive income. In order to realize another capital gain, another asset must be purchased and acquired. As its value rises, it can also be sold to lock in another capital gain. Capital gain investments are generally larger amounts, though they only pay one time.

Capital gains have to be reported to the Internal Revenue Service, whether they belong to a business or an individual. These capital gains have to be designated as either short term gains or long term gains. This is decided by how long you hold the asset before choosing to sell it. When an asset with a gain is held longer than a year, the capital gain is long term. If it is held for a year or less time frame, such a capital gain proves to be short term.

When an individual or business' long term capital gains are greater than long term capital losses, net capital gains exist. This is true to the point that these gains are greater than net short term capital losses. Tax rates on these capital gains are lower than on other forms of income. Up to 2010's conclusion, the highest capital gains tax rates for the majority of investors proves to be fifteen percent. Those whose incomes are lower are taxed at a zero percent rate on their net capital gains.

When capital gains are negative, or are actually capital losses, the losses may be deducted form your tax return. This reduces other forms of income by as much as the yearly limit of $3,000. Additional capital losses can be carried over to future years when they exceed $3,000 in any given year, reducing income for tax purposes in the future. These capital gains and losses should be reported on the IRS' Schedule D for capital gains and losses.

Capital Loss

Capital Loss refers to a type of loss that companies or individuals experience as one of their capital assets decreases by value. This includes a real estate or investment asset. The loss only becomes realized when the asset itself sells for less than the price for which it was originally purchased. Another way of looking at these capital losses is that they represent the difference from the asset's purchase price and the asset's selling price. In other words, for it to be a loss the selling price must be less than the original price. As an example, when investors purchase a home for $300,000 and then sell the same home six years later for only $260,000, they have taken a capital loss amounting to $40,000.

Where income taxes are concerned, capital losses often offset capital gains. Capital losses in fact reduce the personal or business income in a like dollar for dollar amount. When net losses are higher than $3,000, then the overage amount can not be applied. Instead, this amount higher than net $3,000 simply carries over against any other gains or taxable income to the following year when they will similarly offset capital gains and income. When losses are multiple thousands, they continue to carry forward as many years as it takes for them to be fully exhausted.

Both capital losses and capital gains will be reported using a Form 8949. This form helps taxpayers to determine if the sale dates allow for the transactions to be counted as long term or short term losses or gains. When such transactions are deemed to be short term gains, they become taxable by the individual's ordinary income tax rates. These ranged from only 10 percent to 39.6 percent as of 2015. This is why the shorter term losses when paired off against shorter term gains give significant tax advantages to higher income earning individuals. It benefits them when they have earned profits by selling off any asset or assets in under a year from original purchase point.

With longer term capital gains, investors become taxed by rates of zero percent, 15 percent, or 20 percent. This occurs when they take a gain which results from a position they possessed for over a year. Such capital gains also can only be offset by capital losses which they realize after holding the investments for over a year. It is also on form 8949 that these assets become reportable. Here investors list out both the gross proceeds from the sales and assets' cost basis. The two figures are compared to determine if the total sales equate to a loss, gain, or wash. Such losses become reported on Schedule D. Here the taxpayer is able to ascertain the amount that may be utilized to lower overall taxable income.

These wash sale rules can be confusing to individuals without an example. Consider an investor who dumps his IBM stock on the last day of November in order to realize a loss. The taxing authority of the Internal Revenue Service will disallow such a capital loss if the exact stock was bought again on the day of December 30th or before this. This is because investors have to wait at least 31 days before such a security can be repurchased then sold off once more in order to realize another loss.

Yet the regulation does not affect sales and re-buys of different mutual funds that possess similar positions and holdings. As an example, $10,000 worth of Vanguard Energy Fund shares may be entirely reinvested in the Fidelity Select Energy Portfolio at any point. This would not forfeit the investors' ability to recognize another loss even as they continue to own an equity portfolio (through the mutual fund) that is similar to their earlier mutual fund holdings.

Cash Flow

Cash Flow is either an incoming revenue or outgoing expense stream that affects the value of any cash account over time. Inflows of cash, or positive cash flows, typically result from one of three possible activities, including operations, investing, or financing for businesses or individuals. Individuals are also able to realize positive cash flows from gifts or donations.

Negative cash flow is also called cash outflows. Outflows of cash happen because of either expenses or investments made. This is the case for both individuals' finances, as well as for those of businesses.

Where both individual finances and business corporate finances are concerned, positive cash flows are required to maintain solvency. Cash flows could be demonstrated because of a past transaction like selling a business product or a personal item or investment. They might also be projected into a future time for some consideration that a company or individual anticipates receiving and then possibly spending. No person or corporation can survive for long without cash flow.

Positive cash flow is essential for a variety of needs. Sufficient cash flow allows for money for you to pay your personal bills and creditors. It also allows a business to cover the costs of employee payroll, suppliers' bills, and creditors' payments in a timely fashion. When individuals and businesses lack sufficient cash on hand to maintain their budget or operations, then they are named insolvent. Lasting insolvency generally leads to personal or corporate bankruptcy.

For businesses, statements of cash flows are created by accountants. These demonstrate the quantity of cash that is created and utilized by a corporation in a certain time frame. Cash flows in this definition are calculated by totaling net income following taxes with non cash charges like depreciation. Cash flow is able to be assigned to either a business' entire operations or to one particular segment or project of the company. Cash flow is often considered to be an effective measurement of a business' ongoing financial strength.

Cash flows are also used by business and individuals to ascertain the value or return of a project or investment. The numbers of cash flows in to and out of such projects and investments are often utilized as inputs for indicators of performance like net present value and internal rate of return. A problem with a business' liquidity can also be determined by measuring the entire entity's cash flow.

Many individuals prefer investments that yield periodic positive cash flow over ones that pay only one time capital gains. High yielding dividend stocks, energy trusts, and real estate investment trusts are all examples of positive cash flow investments. Real estate properties can also be positive cash flow yielding investments when they provide greater amounts of rental income than their combined monthly mortgage payments, maintenance expenses, and property management upkeep costs and outflows total.

Chapter 11 Bankruptcy

Chapter 11 Bankruptcy proves to be a specific type of bankruptcy. This kind has to do with the business assets, debts, and affairs being reorganized. The business reorganization filing was named for the Section 11 of the United States' Bankruptcy Code. Corporations commonly file it that need some time to rearrange the terms of their debts and their business operations. It gives them a fresh start on repaying their debt obligations. Naturally the indebted company will have to stick to the terms of the reorganization plan. This proves to be the most highly complex type of bankruptcy filing possible. Companies have been advised to only entertain it once they have contemplated their other options and analyzed the repercussions of such a filing.

This Chapter 11 bankruptcy rarely makes the news unless it is a nationally known or famous corporation which is filing. Among the major corporations that have filed such a Chapter 11 bankruptcy are United Airlines, General Motors, K-Mart, and Lehman Brothers. The first three successfully emerged from it and became as great or stronger than they were before falling into hard times financially. In reality, the vast majority of these cases are unknown to the general public. As an example, in the year 2010, nearly 14,000 separate corporations filed for Chapter 11.

The point of this Chapter 11 Bankruptcy is to assist a corporation in restructuring both obligations and debts. The goal is not to close down the business. In fact it rarely leads to the corporation closing. Instead, corporations like K-mart, General Motors, and tens of thousands of others were able to survive and once again thrive thanks to the useful process of protection from creditors and reorganization of business debts.

It is typically LLCs Limited Liability Companies, partnerships, and corporations that make application for Chapter 11 Bankruptcy. There are cases where individuals who are positively saddled with debt and who are not able to be approved for a Chapter 13 or Chapter 7 filing can be qualified for Chapter 11 instead. The time table for successfully completing Chapter 11 bankruptcy ranges from several months to as long as two years.

Businesses that are in the middle of their Chapter 11 cases are encouraged to keep operating. The debtor in possession will typically run the business normally. Where there are cases that have gross incompetence, dishonest dealings, or even fraud involved, typically trustees come in to take over the business and its daily operations while the bankruptcy proceedings are ongoing.

Corporations in the midst of these filings will not be permitted to engage in specific decisions without first having to consult with the courts to proceed. They may not terminate or sign rental agreements, sell any assets beyond regular inventory, or expand existing business operations or alternatively cease them. The bankruptcy court retains full control regarding any hiring and paying of lawyers as well as signing contracts with either unions or vendors. Lastly, such indebted organizations and entities may not sign for a loan that will pay once the bankruptcy process finishes.

After the business or person files their chapter 11 bankruptcy, it gains the right to offer a first reorganization plan. Such plans often include renegotiating owed debts and reducing the company size in order to slash expenses. There are some scenarios where the plan will require every asset to be liquidated in order to pay off the creditors, as with Lehman Brothers.

When plans are fair and workable, courts will approve them. This moves the reorganization process ahead. For plans to be accepted, they also have to maintain the creditors' best interests for the future repayment of debts owed to them. When the debtor can not or will not put forward a plan of their own for reorganization, then the creditors are invited to offer one in the indebted company or person's place.

Chapter 7 Bankruptcy

Chapter 7 bankruptcy is a form of protection from creditors. Unlike Chapter 13 bankruptcy, it does not have any repayment plan. In the Chapter 7 a bankruptcy trustee determines what eligible assets the debtor individual or company has. The trustee then collects these available assets, sells them, and distributes proceeds to the creditors against their debts. This is all done under the rules of the Bankruptcy Code.

Debtors are permitted to keep specific property that is exempt, such as their house. Other property that the debtor holds will be mortgaged or have liens put against it to pledge it to the various creditors until it is liquidated. Debtors who file chapter 7 will likely forfeit property in partial payment of debts.

Chapter 7 bankruptcy is available to corporations, partnerships, and individuals who pass a means test. The relief can be granted whether or not the debtor is ruled to be insolvent.

Chapter 7 bankruptcy cases start when debtors file their petitions with their particular area's bankruptcy court. For businesses, they use the address where the main office is located. Debtors are required to give the court information that includes schedules of current expenditures and income and liabilities and assets.

They are also required to furnish a financial affairs statement and a schedule of contracts and leases which are not expired. The debtors will also have to deliver the trustee tax return copies from the most current tax year along with any tax returns which they file while the case is ongoing.

Debtors who are individuals also have to furnish their court with other documents. They are required to file a credit counseling certificate and any repayment plan created there. They must also file proof of income from employers 60 days before their original filing, a monthly income statement along with expected increases in either, and notice of interest they have in tuition or state education accounts. Husbands and wives are allowed to file individually or jointly. They must abide by the requirements for individual debtors either way.

The courts are required to charge debtors who file $335 in filing, administrative, and trustee fees. Debtors typically pay these when they file to the clerk of court. The court can give permission for individuals to pay by installments instead. When the income of debtor's proves to be less than 150% of the amount of the poverty level, the court can choose to drop the fee requirements.

Debtors will have to provide a great amount of information in order to complete their Chapter 7 filing and receive a discharge of debts. They have to list out each of their creditors along with the amounts they owe then and the type of claim. Debtors have to furnish a list of all property the own. They must also give the information on the amount, source, and frequency of income they have to the court.

Finally, they will be required to provide an in depth list of all monthly living expenses that includes housing, utilities, food, transportation, clothing, medicine, and taxes. This helps the court to determine if the debtor is able to set up a repayment plan instead of discharging the debts.

From 21 to 40 days after the debtor files the petition with the courts, the trustee hosts a creditors' meeting. The debtor will have to cooperate with the trustee on any requests for additional financial documents or records. At this meeting, the trustee will ask questions to make sure the debtor is fully aware of the consequences of debt discharge by the bankruptcy court. Sometimes trustees will deliver this in written form to the debtor before or at the meeting. Assuming the trustee makes the recommendation for discharge, the Federal bankruptcy court judge will discharge the debts when the process is completed.

Collateral

Collateral refers to an asset or piece of Real Estate which borrowers provide as security to lenders in exchange for a loan. This property actually secures the mortgage or other form of loan. In the event that the borrowers do not continue to make the agreed upon payments on the loan according to the laid out schedule, the financial institution has the right to seize this property in order to recover the principal losses.

Because such collateral provides at least nominal security to the lending institution in the scenarios where the borrower refuses to or is unable repay the loan, these forms of loans are commonly provided with lower interest rates as compared to those loans which are unsecured entirely. When such a lender has interest in the underlying property provided by the borrower then this is referred to as a lien.

In the end there are several arrangements with such collateral. The type of loan often determines which form will be required within the contract. With car loans or mortgages, the loans are secured by the property upon which the financial institution issues the loan. Other forms of loans have more flexible security, as with collateralized personal loans. In order for any loan to be called secured, the backing security has to be at least equal to or greater than the balance that remains on the loan in question.

Such secured loans entail far less risk for lenders because the underlying property serves as an incentive for the borrower to keep paying back the loan. Borrowers know all too well that if they do not complete the required payments then the financial institution which holds the loan may legally possess (or repossess) this collateral in order to recoup the money it is owed on the rest of the loan.

With mortgages, the collateral in question will always be the home that the borrower buys using the loan in the first place. If and when they fail to pay the debts, then the lender may seize possession of the property by utilizing a procedure called foreclosure. After the lender completes the necessary court process and has the property back in its possession, it is allowed to sell off the home to someone else. This will permit the bank to cover the principal which remains on the original loan along with their costs for the foreclosure.

Houses also can also be utilized for second mortgage collateral, or against HELOC's (Home Equity Lines of Credit). In such scenarios, the credit delivered by the financial institution may not be greater than the equity which exists within the home itself. As a tangible example, a home could have a market value of $300,000. At the same time, it might be that $175,000 of the original mortgage balance remains to pay. This would mean that the majority of HELOC's or even second mortgages would not exceed the available equity of $125,000.

Collateral is also utilized in margin accounts' trading of stocks, commodities, and futures. In this case, it is the securities themselves that become the property which secures the brokerage loan. In the event that a margin call has to be issued and the account holder will not or can not pay it on demand, then the securities' value ultimately makes certain that the brokerage will get back its loaned money.

Sometimes financial institutions will require additional collateral be put up for a given existing loan, if the contract allows such a scenario. This will reduce increasing risks for the lending institution. A creditor could give notice that without such additional security, they will be forced to raise the interest rate on the loan. Additionally accepted security could be certificates of deposit, cash, equipment, letters of credit, or even shares of stock.

Commodities

Commodities turn out to be items that are taken from the earth, such as orange juice, cattle, wheat, oil, and gold. Companies buy commodities to turn them into usable products like bread, gasoline, and jewelry to sell to other businesses and consumers. Individual investors purchase and sell them for the purposes of speculation, in an attempt to make a profit.

Commodities are traded through commodities brokers on one of several different commodities exchanges, such as COMEX, or the Commodities Mercantile Exchange, NYMEX, or the New York Mercantile Exchange, and NYBOT, or the New York Board of Trade, among others.

Commodities are traded with contracts using a great amount of leverage. This means that with a small amount of money, a great quantity of the commodity in question can be controlled and traded. For example, with only a few thousand dollars, you as an investor are able to control a contract of one thousand barrels of heating oil or one hundred ounces of gold.

As a result of this high leverage that you obtain, the amounts of money made or lost can be significant with only relatively small moves in the price of the underlying commodity. This leverage results from the fact that commodities are nearly always traded using margin accounts that lead to significant risks for the capital invested. For example, with gold contracts, each ten cent minimum price move represents a $10 per contract gain or loss.

Commodity trading strategies center around speculation on factors that will affect the production of a commodity. These could be related to weather, natural disasters, strikes, or other events. If you believed that severe hurricanes would damage a great portion of the Latin American coffee crop, then you would call your commodity broker and instruct them to buy as many coffee contracts as they had money in the account to cover.

If the hurricanes took place and coffee did see significant damage in the region, then the prices of coffee would rise dramatically as a result of the negative weather, causing the coffee harvest to be more valuable. Your coffee contracts would similarly rise in value, probably significantly.

A variety of commodities can be traded on the commodities exchanges. These include grains, metals, energy, livestock, and softs. Grains consistently prove to be among the most popular of commodities available to trade. Grain commodities are usually most active in the spring and summer. Grains include soybeans, corn, oats, wheat, and rough rice.

Metals commodities offer you the opportunity to take positions on precious metals such as gold and silver. Changes in the underlying prices of base metals may also be traded in this category. Metals include copper, silver, and gold.

Energy commodities that you can trade are those used for heating homes and fueling vehicles for the nation. With the energy complex you can trade on supply disruptions around the world or higher gas prices that you anticipate. Energy commodities available to you are crude oil, unleaded gas, heating oil, and natural gas.

Livestock includes animals that provide pork and beef. Because these are staple foods in most American diets, they provide among the more reliable pattern trends for trading. Pork bellies, lean hogs, and live cattle are all examples of tradable livestock commodities.

Softs are comprised of both food and fiber types of commodities. Many of these are deemed to be exotic since they are grown in other countries and parts of the earth. Among the soft markets that you can trade are sugar, coffee, cocoa, cotton, orange juice, and lumber.

Common Stock

Common stocks are shares in an underlying company that represent equity ownership in the corporation. They are also known as ordinary shares. These are securities in which individuals invest their capital. Common stock is the opposite of preferred stock.

While common stock and preferred stock both represent ownership in the company, there are many important differences between the two. Should a company go bankrupt, common stock holders are only given their money after preferred stock owners, bond owners, and creditors. Yet, common stock performs well, typically seeing greater levels of price appreciation than does preferred stock.

Common stock typically comes with voting rights, another feature that preferred stock does not have. These votes are used in electing the board of directors at the company's annual meeting, as well as in determining such things as company strategy, stock splits, policies, mergers and acquisitions, and the sale of the company. Preemptive rights in common stocks refer to owners with these rights being allowed to keep the same proportion of ownership in the company' stock, even if it issues additional stock.

Common stocks do not always pay dividends to share holders, as preferred stocks typically do. The dividends of common stocks are not pre-set or fixed. This means that the dividend returns are not completely predictable. Instead, they are based on a company's reinvestment policies, earnings results, and practices of the market in the valuing of the stock shares themselves.

Common shares have various other benefits. They are typically less expensive than are preferred stock shares. They are more heavily traded and readily available as well. The spreads between the buying and selling prices on them tend to be tighter as a result. Common stocks generally provide capital appreciation as the price of the shares rises over time, assuming that the company continues to do well and meet or exceed expectations. Dividends are often paid to common share holders when these things prove to be the case.

Common stocks can be purchased in any denominated amount. Round lots of common stocks are sold by even one hundred share amounts. This means that five hundred shares of common stock would be considered to be five lots of common stock.

Common stocks represent principally capital gains types of investments, as an investor is looking to buy them low and sell them at a higher price. This leads to a capital gain when the stock is sold at this greater level. The capital gain is the difference between the selling price and the purchasing price. Common stocks can also be cash flow types of investments when they pay a reliable stream of dividends every quarter. These income amounts are typically smaller than the one time amounts realized in capital gains, though they are obtained four times per year on a quarterly basis, or occasionally more often on a monthly basis.

Compound Interest

Compound interest represents interest which calculates on both the original principal amount as well as the interest that was accumulated previously during the loan or investment. Economists have called this miraculous phenomenon an interest on interest. It causes loans or invested deposits to increase at a significantly faster pace than only simple interest, the opposite of compound interest. Simple interest proves to be interest that calculates on just the principal amount of money.

Compound interest accrues at an interest rate which determines how often the compounding occurs. The higher the compound interest rate turns out to be, the faster the principal will compound and the more compounding periods will occur. Consider an example of how effective compounding truly is. $100 that is compounded at a rate of 10% per year will turn out to be less than $100 which is compounded at only 5% but semi annually during the same length of time.

Compound interest is important to individuals as it is able to take a few dollars worth of savings now and transform them into significant money throughout lifetimes. Investors do not need an MBA or a Wall Street background in order to benefit from this principle. Practically all investments earn compounding interest if the owners leave these earnings in the investment account over the long term.

This form of interest cuts both ways on the receiving and paying sides. When individuals are saving and investing money, it helps them grow the amount faster. When they are borrowing and paying the same interest on the debt, it grows against them faster. Individuals who are saving wish their money to compound as often as they can. Individuals who are borrowing wish it to compound as infrequently as possible. Savers are better off if they are able to compound quarterly instead of annually while just the opposite is true for borrowers.

For people who are compounding their investments, time works on their side. Money that grows at a rate of 6% each year doubles every 12 years. This means that it increases to four times as much as the original amount in only 24 years. For individuals paying compound interest, time is similarly working against them. Credit card companies utilize this principle to keep their card owners in debt forever by encouraging them to only make minimum monthly payments on the bills.

Thanks to compounding, a smaller amount of money that a person adds to an account upfront is more valuable than a larger sum of money he or she adds decades later. This cuts both ways. By paying down principal on a credit card with an extra $5 per month, the amount of compound interest individuals pay on a 14% interest rate credit card decreases by $1,315 over ten years. This is true even though they have paid only $600 in extra payments over this amount of time.

Anyone can make the miracle of compounding work for them. The idea works the same whether individuals are investing $100 or $100 million instead. Millionaires have greater ranges of investment choices. Even relatively poor people can compound their interest to increase their original amount and double their money as often as possible.

Compounding interest means that participants have to give up using some dollars today in order to obtain a greater benefit from them in the future. The little money may be missed now, but the rewards for the more significant amounts in the future will more than make up for the little sacrifice the individual makes now. Financial planners have claimed that the difference between poverty and financial comfort in the future amounts to even a few dollars in savings each week invested now rather than later.

Consumer Price Index (CPI)

The Consumer Price Index, also known by its acronym of CPI, actually measures changes that take place over time in the level of the pricing of various consumer goods and services that American households buy. The Bureau of Labor Statistics in the U.S. says that the Consumer Price Index is a measurement of the over time change in the prices that urban consumers actually pay for a certain grouping of consumer goods and services.

This consumer price index is not literal in the sense of what inflation really turns out to be. Instead, it is a statistical estimate that is built utilizing the costs of a basket of sample items that are supposed to be representative for the entire economy. These goods and services' prices are ascertained from time to time. In actual practice, both sub indices such as clothing, and even sub-sub indices, such as men's dress shirts, are calculated for varying sub-categories of services and goods. These are then taken and added together to create the total index. The different goods are assigned varying weights as shares of the total amount of the expenditures of consumers that the index covers.

Two essential pieces of information are necessary to build the consumer price index. These are the weighting data and the pricing data. Weighting data comes from estimates of differing kinds of expenditure shares as a percentage of the entire expenditure that the index covers. Sample household expenditure surveys are sourced to figure what the weightings should be. Otherwise, the National Income and Product Accounts estimates of expenditures on consumption are utilized. Pricing data is gathered from a sampling of goods and services taken from a sample range of sales outlets in varying locations and at a sampling of times.

The consumer price index is figured up monthly in the United States. Some other countries determine their CPI's on a quarterly basis. The different components of the consumer price index include food, clothing, and housing, all of which are weighted averages of the sub-sub indices. The CPI index literally compares the prices of one month with the prices in the reference month.

Consumer Price Index is only one of a few different pricing indices that the majority of national statistical agencies calculate. Inflation is figured up using the yearly percentage changes in the underlying consume price index. Uses of this CPI can include adjusting real values of pensions, salaries, and wages for inflation's effects, as well as for monitoring costs, and showing alterations in actual values through deflating the monetary magnitudes. The CPI and US National Income and Product Accounts prove to be among the most carefully followed of economic indicators.

Cost of living index is another measurement that is generated based on the consumer price index. It demonstrates how much consumer expenditures need to adjust to compensate for changes in prices. This details how much consumers need to keep up a constant standard of living.

Core Inflation

Core Inflation refers to the change in the cost of goods and services without calculating the important categories of food and energy. The U.S. federal government believes this to be the most accurate means of figuring up true inflationary trends. They claim that both energy products and food components are priced too volatilely to be a part of the core inflation calculation and figure. This is because they constantly change so rapidly that they interfere with inflation readings.

The reason for this is that they are subject to the whims of the traders on the various commodity market exchanges. The majority of core food products like beef, pork, wheat, orange juice, and more and energy products such as oil, natural gas, and gasoline trade each and every week day all throughout the day.

As an example, traders of commodities will likely bid up the prices of oil and its derivative products when they believe its supplies will diminish or if they feel that demand will outpace supplies. It could be that a strike will interrupt production and oil supplies from Nigeria, Venezuela, or Angola. Because of this fear, traders will purchase oil at the prices today and hope to sell it for a higher amount at the anticipated greater prices tomorrow or next week.

That is all that it really takes to radically increase the price of oil. Should the strike wrap up quickly, then the oil prices will plunge when traders suddenly all sell out of their positions. This is why both energy and food prices depend on rapidly changing human emotions rather than real changes to underlying forces of supply and demand. Between this and the inelastic demand of food and energy which people simply have to possess in order to live, these commodities rise and fall crazily sometimes.

Consider how gasoline prices will change when their primary input oil does. Yet as people require gas to travel to school and work, they cannot delay their purchases and wait for prices to decline. Food prices also vary according to gasoline and oil prices as they are shipped by truck throughout the United States. In truth, most foods on your dinner plate have more frequent flyer miles than you ever dreamed of acquiring.

The Fed has a few tools to deal with higher than desired core inflation. The problem comes with their tools needing time to take effect on the broader economy. This might mean as much as from six to 18 months before changes to the Fed Funds rate will show a meaningful impact on the inflation rate in the U.S. As the Fed Funds rate goes higher, so will the bank loans and mortgage rates. Credit will tighten and slow economic growth. Corporations find themselves lowering their core prices in order to keep selling merchandise. This lowers inflation as it finally all feeds through to the economy.

The Federal Reserve targets inflation with their policies. They promise to not take action when the core inflation rate remains at two percent or lower. Consider a real world example. Inflation has a tendency to creep higher throughout the summer as people go on vacations. The Fed does not wish to raise rates each summer though, which would force them to proportionally lower them again in the fall.

Rather, they wait and see if such summer increases boost the prices of the goods and services ex food and energy permanently. Yet ultimately higher food and gas prices force up the prices of all other goods and services if they remain elevated for long. This is why the Federal Reserve will also consider the headline inflation rate, which is the opposite of the core inflation rate. This broader measure of inflation considers food and energy prices alongside all other goods and services.

The core inflation rate can be measured via the Core Price Index, or core CPI, as well as the core Personal Consumption Expenditures price index, or core PCE price index.

Corporation

A corporation refers to a business entity where it is distinctive and separated from the owners. Such corporations may take on many responsibilities similar to individuals. They can borrow and loan out money, make and execute contracts, hire and terminate employees, sue or become sued, pay taxes, and own cash and assets. This is why corporations are many times referred to by the phrase of legal person.

A corporation is a legal construct that controls and runs businesses of all types all over the globe. There may be differing legal arrangements from one government jurisdiction to the next, but they all have the attribute of a limited liability. With this protection, shareholders enjoy important rights like benefitting from dividends as a result of profits and price appreciation from successful business endeavors. While enjoying these advantages, limited liability means that they do not carry any of the personal responsibility for payment of the company's debts.

Practically every famous business and brand in the world is a part of a corporation. This includes such internationally recognized entities as Coca-Cola, McDonalds, Microsoft, and Toyota Motors. Corporations can also do business under a different name. A classic example of this is Alphabet Inc. that runs Google.

Corporations are established as a group of stock holders choose to incorporate. They pursue this follow up after a common goal in their ownership of the business. Such corporations may be charitable as well as for profit. The overwhelming majority of such companies are founded with the ambition of earning positive returns for the stock holders. These shareholders own some percentage of the corporation in exchange for paying for their shares. If they obtain them directly from the company, then their payments remit to the treasury of the company itself.

Corporations sometimes possess thousands of shareholders, especially when they are publicly traded companies. These entities could also have only a few or even one shareholder. The most common corporations within the United States are called "C Corporations."

Shareholders use their one vote per share to vote for the company board of directors every year. This group is responsible for naming the management which they oversee. The managers run the daily activities of the company. It is the corporation's board of directors which must carry out the business plan of the entity. They also do not bear responsibility for the company's debts, but have a fiduciary responsibility to care for the corporation. If they do not fulfill the duty faithfully, they may become personally liable for mistakes. There are tax statutes that allow for board of directors members to be personally liable.

As these corporations fulfill their goals, they can be wound down through a process also known as liquidation. In this process, they appoint a liquidator to sell off the company assets, pay the creditors, and share out all cash assets which remain among the stockholders. This can be done as a result of an involuntary or a voluntary procedure. Creditors can force liquidation when a company can no longer pay its debts. This often leads to corporate bankruptcy.

Credit Bureaus

Credit bureaus are agencies that collect financial information. They go by different names in various countries around the world. In the United Kingdom they are known as credit reference agencies. In Australia, the bureaus are called credit reporting bodies. India knows their credit agencies as credit information companies.

Within the United States, these organizations are called consumer reporting agencies. Whatever name they go by, they all serve the same function. The bureaus gather information from banks and other financial sources to deliver consumer credit information about individual consumers.

The U.S. consumer reporting agencies are governed by the Fair Credit Reporting Act. Other laws that regulate the activities of the bureaus are the Fair and Accurate Credit Transactions Act, the Fair Credit Billing Act, the Fair Credit Reporting Act, and Regulation B. These acts attempt to safeguard consumers against unfair practices and mistakes made by the data providers and the credit reporting agencies themselves.

The U.S. has two separate government organizations who oversee the credit bureaus and their data suppliers. These are the FTC and the OCC. Primary oversight of the credit reporting agencies as they deal with consumers belongs to the Federal Trade Commission. The banks are monitored for all of the information that they provide the reporting agencies by the Office of the Controller of the Currency. This government agency supervises, regulates, and charters all of the national banks and any information they turn over to the consumer credit reporting agencies.

Three main credit reporting bureaus dominate nearly all credit reporting in the U.S. These are Experian, Equifax, and TransUnion. None of these three agencies are owned by government entities. All of them exist as companies seeking to make a profit and are traded publically. They are carefully monitored for fairness by the government provided oversight organizations.

The consumer reporting agencies operate through a vast network with the credit card issuing companies, banks, and other financial entities with which individuals have accounts. All of these ties ensure that credit account information and histories show up on the credit reports of one, two, or even all of the bureaus.

The credit bureaus compile all of this information into a consumer credit report. They each then utilize proprietary trade secret formulas to determine every individual's FICO credit score. Each of the three bureaus formulates its own score that is different from that of its competitors. They also come up with educational credit score numbers which are often vastly different from the official scores.

Consumers do not have to settle for educational credit scores. They have the rights to see what is on their credit reports. Each and every year, individuals are able to obtain an official credit report from each of the three credit bureaus. This can be done by going to the government mandated website AnnualCreditReport.com.

Besides this, consumers are allowed to go to the websites of the three main consumer reporting agencies and order credit reports and scores from them directly. The only way to get the official credit score is to pay for and order it from the credit bureaus themselves. These are not provided in the annual free reports. Experian and Equifax offer all three credit reports in a single convenient to view document.

Sometimes the credit bureaus will make mistakes with individuals' credit reports. When this happens, it is important to get in touch with the credit bureau itself in order to dispute any information that is inaccurate. These organizations also should be contacted directly if there is concern about fraud so that they can place a security alert or fraud alert on the person's credit report.

Credit Ratings Agencies

Credit Ratings Agencies are those companies whose purpose is to consider and report on the financial strength which firms and government agencies demonstrate. They report on national as well as international corporations and agencies in this capacity. Their reports are most interested in the ability of the entities in question to fulfill their obligations for both principal and interest repayments of their bonds and other kinds of debts. Besides this, the various ratings agencies carefully examine and review the conditions and terms on every debt issue.

The end result of the agencies' work is to release a credit rating on both the debt issues in particular and the debt issuers more generally. When they agencies have high confidence that the issuer will be able to meet their debt servicing of principal and interest as promised, they will issue a high credit rating. When the opposite is true, the credit rating will be lower. It is entirely possible for a particular issue of debt to receive a differing credit rating from the issuer. This heavily depends on the particular terms of the issuer.

The impacts of these debt issue ratings are enormous in the industry and for the specific issuers in question. Those debt issues that obtain the best credit ratings will receive the most attractive interest rates from the credit markets. This is because the confidence of investors in an entity's capability of making their various payment obligations comes down to the credit ratings agencies review, analyses and especially ratings. Since the interest rates which investors demand for a specific debt issue will be inversely correlated to the borrower's particular creditworthiness, weaker borrowers will have to pay more while the stronger ones will enjoy paying less.

In this way, the credit ratings agencies act on behalf of businesses in much the same capacity as the consumer credit bureaus do for individual consumers. Such credit scores which the credit bureaus develop for individual people will greatly impact the interest rates at which individuals are able to borrow money.

The downside to these credit ratings agencies and their work is that they have been made the scapegoat for company and government defaults in recent years. Their research quality in particular has been the target of heavy criticism from observers and analysts who point out companies which they rated highly suddenly collapsed. Governments in Europe on which they provided high credit ratings defaulted or almost defaulted on their debts, as with Greece in particular.

This caused third party observers to argue that the various credit ratings agencies are actually poor at financial forecasting, at uncovering growing and negative trends for the debt issuers they follow, and also are overly late in revising down their ratings. Besides this, critics point to the many conflicts of interest of the ratings agencies. This is because the debt issuers are able to pick out and pay the ratings agencies for the reviews of their bonds. In a survey conducted in 2008, 11 percent of the various investment professionals surveyed by the CFA Institute responded that they had observed personally instances where the major ratings agencies had actually upgraded their given ratings on bonds when they were pressured by the debt issuers in question.

There are only three firms today which dominate the space, and this is part of the problem. The Wall Street Journal provided the ratings shares of the big 3 agencies in their 2011 report. Of the 2.8 million ratings they issue collectively (with the other seven minor agencies), S&P 500 controls the greatest market share with 42.2 percent. Moody's holds 36.9 percent of the market. Fitch rounds out the top three with 17.9 percent.

The article claimed that fully 95 percent of all revenues in this industry were earned by the big three. Only 2.9 percent of the ratings issued came from the other seven firms. The other seven credit ratings agencies were A.M. Best, DBRS, Japan Credit Rating Agency, Rating and Investment Info., Egan-Jones Ratings, Morningstar Credit Ratings, and Kroll Bond Rating Agency.

Between the top two issuers Moody's and Standard & Poor's, they provide ratings for roughly 80 percent of all municipal and corporate bond issues. They are typically regarded as a level higher than Fitch. One particular example speaks volumes. While Egan-Jones had downgraded the U.S. Federal government debt to the second highest rating years earlier, it was ignored largely by the markets and world. When Standard & Poor's took the same action by downgrading the Federal government of the United States debt to AA+ on August 5th of 2011, this shook the world bond, currency, and stock markets. It demonstrates the clout S&P and Moody's especially enjoy over all of their various credit ratings agencies rivals.

Creditor

Creditors are those financial institutions or individuals who extend credit to a business or other individual. They carry this out by providing financing which they expect will be paid back at a set time in the future. There is another type of creditor as well. This is a company which delivers services or supplies to a person or other business yet does not insist on immediate payment. Since the customer actually does owe the company money for the goods or services provided in advance of payment, that company becomes their creditor de facto.

Within the universe of a creditor there are real and personal categories of them. Finance companies and banks represent real creditor situations. This is because they possess official and legally binding contracts which they sign with the borrower. In this action, they bind assets of the borrower as collateral against the loan in many cases. Typical collateral would be the underlying asset for which the borrower is obtaining credit in the first place. This is often a car, a house, or some other piece of Real Estate. A personal creditor is a family member of friend choosing to loan out money to their loved one or friend.

Real creditors do not loan out money out of the goodness of their hearts. Instead, they intend to earn profits by charging the borrowers interest for these loans. Looking at an example helps to clarify the concept. A creditor might loan out $10,000 to a borrower at a six percent rate of interest. The lending institution will realize earnings in the form of loan interest.

For this accommodation, the creditor is taking on some amount of risk that the borrowing business or individual might potentially default on the loan. This is why the majority of those extending credit will price the interest rate which they charge the borrower based on the business or persons' prior credit history and creditworthiness. It becomes important to borrowers of especially large amounts of money to have high credit quality so that they are able to obtain a more advantageous interest rate and save money on the interest payments.

The rates of interest on mortgages depend heavily on a host of different variables. Some of these are the nature of the lender, the credit history of the borrower, and the amount of the upfront down payment. Still, it is usually the creditworthiness that overwhelmingly determines the final interest rate which becomes applied to a loan such as a mortgage. This is because those borrowers who boast fantastic credit histories and scores come across as low risk for the creditor in question. It is why they enjoy the lowest of interest rates. As lower credit score-carrying borrowers prove to be considerably riskier for the creditors, they manage their risk by requiring a greater rate of interest in compensation.

There are cases where a creditor will not obtain repayment. In such cases, they do have several options. Banks and official real credit issuing entities are allowed to repossess the underlying collateral. This would mean they have the ability to seize either the car or home which secured the loan. Where unsecured debts are concerned, it is more difficult to collect. They might sue the borrower for the unpaid debts in these cases. Courts could choose to issue orders attempting to force the borrower to pay them back. They might do this by seizing assets in their bank accounts or by garnishing their wages with their employers.

Sometimes the borrowers will choose to file for bankruptcy. In these cases, the courts will be the ones to alert the creditor to the situation. There are cases where any non- necessary assets can be liquidated so that debts can be paid back. The order of priority will make unsecured creditors last in the receiving line.

Crypto Currency

A crypto currency turns out to be a virtual currency. These alternative currencies deploy cryptography as a means of security. It makes them extremely hard to counterfeit since this security feature is complex. An element that consistently defines the various crypto currencies and simultaneously endears them to users is their independent nature. They cannot be issued nor controlled by any of the global central banks or world monetary authorities. The theory is that this makes it difficult (if not outright impossible) for governments to manipulate or control such currencies.

Unfortunately for the governments of the world, this somewhat anonymous characteristic of the global crypto currencies also makes them an ideal vehicle for illegal and otherwise unethical activities. Among these are drug dealing, tax evading, and money laundering carried on around the world.

The world's original (and still leading) crypto currency proved to be Bitcoin. This was the first of the alternative currencies that caught on with the general and investing public. A mysterious individual or group of individuals who go only by the pseudonym of Satoshi Nakamoto created and launched Bitcoin back in 2009. These BTC (as they are abbreviated) must be mined in a tedious process which involves solving complex computer algorithmic problems. There is a maximum limit of 21 million to the total number of BTC which may be created. As of September of 2015, already 14.6 million of these Bitcoins had been mined and were circulating. The success of Bitcoin has been so vast that other competing crypto currencies have been spawned over the years.

The greatest and most successful of these is Ethereum, or Ether tokens. Others that have appeared include Litecoin, PPCoin, and Namecoin. These descendants of Bitcoin are often referred to as altcoins. This name is a derivative of the phrase bitcoin alternative. All of these crypto currencies have at least one thing in common. They all rely on a decentralized control. This stands out in direct contrast to the centralized banking systems of the mainstream traditional currencies.

There are a number of advantages and also some disadvantages to the major crypto currencies and this ground breaking technology. On the positive side, the crypto currencies enable simpler, cheaper, faster transfers of funds between one party and another in a commercial transaction. The transfers of funds occur utilizing both private and public keys to provide greater security.

The transfers happen with the lowest of possible processing and transaction costs. This has disrupted traditional banking and finance significantly. Individuals who transact in a crypto currency are able to side step the hefty middle man fee of financial institutions such as banks with their wire transfer costs, or with money transfer services like Western Union and Money Gram. These last two services charge upwards of ten percent transfer fees.

The great brilliance of Bitcoin and the other major crypto currencies lies in their block chain technology which acts as storage for the transaction ledger online. In fact all transactions in the BTC technology and currency which have ever happened are maintained in the block chain ledger database. Major banks like JP Morgan Chase have already invested heavily in initiatives to reduce the transaction costs of payment processing and transfers utilizing especially the up and coming Ethereum crypto currency.

This does not mean that there are not downsides to the crypto currencies. As they lack a central offline repository, the balance of an online wallet can be completely wiped out by either the invasion of hackers who steal it or the advent of a single computer crash if owners do not backup their holdings with data copies. There is also the negative of the wildly gyrating volatility in the currencies, which can easily swing up or down by even ten or twenty percent in a single trading session or week. There have also been more than 40 instances of online hacking theft of the various Bitcoin exchanges and companies in the short decade of Bitcoin history.

Deed

A Deed refers to a legal document which allows for a real estate ownership transfer from one party to another. Within the document will always be the names of the new and old owners of the property as well as the legally binding description of said real estate. The document must be signed over by the individual who is selling the property to the buyer.

It is impossible to transfer ownership of a piece of real estate unless you have a document in writing. This is nearly always the deed. Interestingly enough, there is not simply one type of these deeds. There are quitclaim, warranty, grant, and transfer on death kinds of deeds in existence. Each of them has their own reason of use.

Quitclaim deeds are what many individuals regard as basic deeds. They simply transfer over any ownership stake an individual may have in a given property. These do not define the full percentage of the receiver's interest in the property however. They are often utilized by couples getting divorced. One of the aggrieved parties signs off on his or her full rights in the married couple's joint properties to the other party. This is particularly helpful when a lack of clarity exists on an interest in a property that one of the owners (like a spouse) has in his or her name. Quitclaims never absolve the forfeiting party from the co- responsibilities of the mortgage however.

These Quitclaim deeds are also employed when title searches discover that a prior owner or heir to an estate possesses a partial claim on the real estate in question. That individual is able to sign off on such a quitclaim deed in order to allow for the transfer of whatever interest remains to them in the said property.

Warranty deeds provide ownership transfer along with a good guarantee that the transferring party possesses clean title on the real estate. This means that the purchaser can have confidence in the property being completely free of ownership claims or liens. These deeds deliver a guarantee from the sellers that they will provide compensation to the purchasers should this pledge prove to be incorrect. It is also possible for warranty deeds to provide other guarantees that address other potential issues with the real estate transfer transaction.

Grant deeds are those kinds that imply certain pledges along with transferring the ownership of title to the property. These pledges might include that the title is not encumbered or has not previously transferred over to someone else.

Finally, TOD Transfer on Death deeds are much like regular formats of deeds. Their critical difference is that they only go into effect when the owner of the property in question dies. In other words, they permit property holders to will real estate to an heir without having to become involved in proceedings in probate court. Upon death, the deed-named beneficiary will immediately assume ownership of the real estate. This avoids any and all delays and probate paperwork.

Creating such TOD deeds is not any more difficult than completing normal deeds. The owner simply designates the beneficiary, signs said deed, has it notarized, and records it with the appropriate property records office for the given jurisdiction. Such deeds are permitted in 23 different states. These include Wyoming, Wisconsin, Washington, Virginia, South Dakota, Oregon, Oklahoma, Ohio, North Dakota, New Mexico, Nevada, Nebraska, Montana, Missouri, Minnesota, Kansas, Indiana, Illinois, Hawaii, Washington District of Columbia, Colorado, Arkansas, and Arizona.

Deeds are required by law to first be notarized (and sometimes also witnessed) before being filed in the area public records office. The appropriate local records office is typically called either a Land Registry Office, County Recorder's Office, or Register of Deeds. This office is typically located within the county courthouse.

Deficit

Deficits are shortfalls in government revenues that result from them spending more money than they bring in from revenues. The deficit of a government is measurable by including or excluding the interest it pays for its debt. Primary deficit is simply the difference in all taxes and revenues less the present level of government outlays. Conversely, total deficits, usually simply referred to as the deficit, prove to be all spending along with payments on the interest of the debt less the revenues coming in from taxes.

Such fiscal deficits also expand and contract as a result of changing trends in economics. As an example, higher amounts of economic activity in a nation give greater revenues in taxes to the Federal Government. At the same time, economic downturns generally cause a government to increase its levels of expenditures in order to boost spending on unemployment benefits and other types of social insurance programs.

The amount of public debt is also impacted significantly by the amounts of social benefits funded, alterations in the tax code or tax rates, methods of enforcing tax policies, and various additional decisions made with government policies. In other countries that have tremendous energy natural resources such as oil and natural gas, including Saudi Arabia, Russia, Norway, and other nations who are a part of the OPEC, or Organization of Petroleum Exporting Countries, these incomes form the energy sources have an enormous impact on the national finances.

Another impact on the real tangible value of a government deficit, or debt, comes from the amounts of inflation in a country. Over time, inflation lowers the real currency value of such debt. The downsides to inflation result in a government having to pay greater interest rate levels on its debts. This causes public coffers borrowing to become more expensive.

Government deficits are comprised of two main parts. These are cyclical deficits and structural deficits. Cyclical deficits result from any and all extra borrowing that a government has to engage in during the low point of a business cycle. This comes from higher unemployment levels. As unemployment rises, tax receipts fall and expenditures on things like social security inversely rise. The implied definition of cyclical deficits is that they will be completely repaid in the next cyclical peak. This is because a surplus in revenues will exist as taxes rises and spending is lower.

Structural deficits instead represent deficits that are constant regardless of the economic cycle. This results from the overall government expenditure levels being unsustainable in light of the current tax rates. The overall budget deficit is then figured by adding the structural deficit to the cyclical surplus or deficit that exists. Although this is the mainstream distinction between the types of deficits, there are economists who say that the differences between the structural and cyclical deficits are impossible to determine. They contend that cyclical deficits simply can not be measured properly.

Deflation

Deflation is simply the prices of goods and services going down in a given time frame. Deflation is the opposite of inflation, which is the rising cost of goods and services over a period of time. This does not make deflation a good thing in the long run.

Another way of defining deflation is the increasing value of money versus various economic goods over a span of time. With inflation, money is becoming less valuable versus goods over time. Deflation happens as a result of the interaction of four factors. On the one hand, the supply of money in circulation might decline. At the same time, supplies of available goods might increase. The need for goods could drop as well. Finally, the demand for money could go up. If any of these four things happen either separately or in concert, deflation is commonly the result.

The easiest way for deflation to occur is as the supply of goods available on the market goes up at a more rapid pace than does the supply of money. The combination of these elements explains how some goods' costs go up while the costs of others go down at the same time. Despite this, deflation can pose certain problems.

The majority of economists today concur that deflation proves to be both a symptom of economic problems as well as a malaise in and of itself. Some buy into the concepts of good and bad deflation. Good deflation happens as companies are consistently capable of manufacturing goods for cheaper and lower prices because of gains in productivity and other ways of reducing costs. This type of deflation permits a strong and growing GDP growth, with lower unemployment, and rising profits.

Bad deflation is more challenging to grasp. Bad deflation rises as a result of the central bank, or the Federal Reserve, choosing to revalue the country's currency. Or, you could say that the supply of money declining results in this negative form of deflation.

The actual problem that deflation causes is that it creates uncertainty for businesses and their relationships. As a rule, business thrives on confidence and falters on the unknown. Borrowers have to make loan payments that turn out to be greater and greater amounts of purchasing power in deflationary time periods. All the while, the value of the asset that you purchased with the loan is declining. In these circumstances, many borrowers elect to default on the loan and its payments.

A declining spiral similarly exists in deflationary periods. Since businesses begin to enjoy fewer profits, they decide to reduce their employment roles. Individuals do not spend as much money as a result. Businesses then realize smaller profits and again cut back. This degenerates into a vicious cycle down before long, as it becomes self reinforcing. Consumers learn that larger ticket items such as houses and cars will actually cost less in the future and then delay their purchases.

Though deflation has been discussed as a potential problem for the U.S. economy with the economic downturn, the reality is far different. At the same time, from 2006 to 2009, the Federal Reserve massively increased the money supply by more than three hundred percent. This argues not for deflation in the United States' future, but for inflation instead.

Delinquency

Delinquency refers to primarily an individual (but also conceivably an entity or business) failing to make good on what was expected of them according to their duty or the law. It often pertains to failing to affect the minimum due payment or carry out a fiduciary responsibility. An individual who practices Delinquency is called a delinquent. These persons have contractually undertaken obligations to turn in payments on loan accounts according to a pre-arranged routine deadline.

This might include minimum monthly amounts of money owed on a car payment, a credit card payment, or a mortgage payment. As the individuals do not make these payments on time, they become delinquent. When mortgage holders become delinquent, the financial institutions holding the loans are able to start working through foreclosure processes. They will do this when the mortgage account stays unpaid for a specific length of time.

There are many different types of accounts on which people fall into Delinquency. This could be retail account payments, income taxes, mortgages, lines of credit, and more. Individuals who become delinquent suffer the consequences for these financial actions. Such impacts vary with the kind of Delinquency, cause, and length of time it has continued in this unfortunate state. As individuals become late on credit card bills, they can be charged late fees. Those who do not make their required tax payments can have their wages garnered or even their bank account levied by the Internal Revenue Service.

Besides these financial Delinquencies, there are responsibilities which when they are not carried out can be labeled delinquent. By not carrying out one's fiduciary duties, professional responsibilities, or other contractual obligations as set forth by custom or the law, individuals can be called delinquents as well. Police officers who do not professionally carry out their responsibilities to protect ordinary citizens in the line of duty can be found to be delinquent.

It is important not to confuse Delinquency with default. Individuals are officially delinquent at the point when they miss making a required payment of some sort in a timely fashion. By contrast, loan defaults happen as borrowers do not pay back a loan according to the terms on which they agreed to in their original contract. Loans can stay in the delinquent stage without being treated as in default for an unspecified amount of time. The amount of time this remains delinquent rather than in default varies considerably from one creditor and financial institution to another. For example, with student loans, the United States' Federal Government permits these to be fully delinquent for as long as 270 consecutive days before they become considered to be in default.

The U.S. keeps track of its various national Delinquency rates. Per the year 2016 in the fourth quarter, such Delinquencies amounted to 4.15 percent for real estate loans on residential loans, 2.15 percent on loans for consumer credit cards, and .85 percent for real estate loans on commercial loans. The government also maintains official statistics for these rates by year of loan issued. For 2016, this amounted to 2.04 percent, which was near the historically typical average.

The devastating global financial crisis and U.S. mortgage crisis which erupted in 2007 caused the rates to spike to a high in the Great Recession years which reached fully 7.4 percent in the year 2010 in its first quarter. For residential real estate, the rate topped out at 11.26 percent for these specific types of loans. Up to the year 2008 in its second quarter these Delinquencies had not been higher than three percent all the way back to the year 1994 in its first quarter.

Derivative

In the financial world, derivatives are agreements between two different parties that contain values that are dependent on the price movements of an asset, as anticipated in the future, to which they are linked.

This asset, which might be a currency, stock price, or other element is referred to as the underlying. Derivatives are also alternative investments and financial instruments, of which they are numerous kinds. The most common forms of derivatives are futures, swaps, and options.

Investors use derivatives for many different activities. These include for gaining leverage on an investment so that when a small movement occurs in the value of the underlying, they can realize a great gain in the derivative value.

They may also be employed for speculation to profit from, assuming that the underlying asset value goes in the direction that they anticipate. Businesses might similarly hedge their risks in an underlying through opening a derivative contract that moves conversely to their position in the underlying, canceling all or part of the risk in the process. Investors similarly are capable of gaining exposure to an underlying that does not have a tradable instrument associated with it, like with a weather derivative.

Investors can also utilize derivatives to give themselves the ability to create options in which the derivative value is associated with a particular event or condition being met.

Derivatives principally remain a means of offering hedging insurance, allowing one party to lessen their risk exposure while the other reduces a different kind of risk exposure. Derivatives examples of transferring risk are helpful to consider. Millers and wheat farmers might create a derivative by signing a futures contract. This could specify a certain dollar value of money in exchange for a particular quantity of wheat to be exchanged at a future time. In this case, the two parties have actually diminished their risk for the future. The miller is not exposed to possible shortages of wheat, while the farmer is saved from the possible variances in price.

Risk is not completely eliminated in this example since the derivative contract will not cover events that the contract does not mention in particular, like weather conditions. There is similarly a danger that one of the parties will default on their part of the contract. To mitigate these problems, clearing houses insure many futures contracts, although not every such derivative is insured for the risk of counter party default.

Another way of looking at derivatives in this example is that while they reduce one form of risk, they actually present another one. The miller and farmer both pick up another risk by signing off on this contract. For the farmer, the danger lies in the fact that although he is saved from declines in the price of wheat, he is also exposed to the possibility that wheat prices will rise above the set amount in the contract, costing him extra income that he might have obtained. The miller also picks up a risk that the cost of wheat will drop below the amount that he has locked in with this contract.

Disposable Income

Disposable income proves to be the remaining income after an individual has met all of his or her income tax obligations. It is utilized as a means of ascertaining the health of an entire society, as well as a person's general economic condition. Disposable income also turns out to be among the main measurements for determining personal wealth.

Although they are sometimes used interchangeably, disposable income should not be confused with discretionary income. Discretionary income is simply any income that remains following paying the taxes and other customary living expenses. This means that the value for disposable income is a greater amount than discretionary income proves to be in practically every case. Still disposable income does not really deal with the day to day costs of living that people encounter in their normal lives.

For you as an American, disposable income typically proves to be anywhere from ten to fifteen percent of the personal income of an individual. All of the rest of the money goes into one of a number of different taxes. Naturally, this would be individually determined as a result of the amount of income that you have, the withholding allowances that you enjoy, and the state in which you reside. Similarly, for other countries, disposable income can be figured more or less by examining the typical tax rates.

Disposable income commonly decreases in difficult economic times, such as recessions and depressions. This does not happen because of an increase in taxes. Instead, it is more a factor of the likelihood of it falling in challenging economic times as companies cut back on employee payrolls. Because of this, lower disposable income will mean that people have more difficult times in fulfilling their present obligations. This will make them far less likely to take on new financial responsibilities.

When people do not make enough money to be taxed, then their disposable income may actually prove to be about the same as their total income is. This is similarly the case in nations that do not charge their citizens personal income taxes. In such cases, gross income and disposable income are identical.

Besides being used for spending on needs and expenses, it can also be saved and invested. Through wisely purchasing cash flow investments with disposable income, the resulting disposable income in the future can actually be consistently higher as regular investment income comes in to the person's account. Disposable income used for capital gains investments will commonly lead to one time gains on sales, which will only temporarily increase disposable income for one time.

Diversifying

Diversifying refers to the means of effectively lowering your investing risk by putting your money into a wide range of various assets. A truly well diversified portfolio offers the benefits of lower amounts of risk than those that are simply invested into one or two asset classes or kinds of investments.

Everyone should engage in some amount of diversification, even if the individual proves to be one who is tolerant of risk. Those individuals who really fear the present day economic uncertainties and very real amounts of risk in the market place will perform better forms of diversification into more asset groups.

Mainstream diversification is always recommended by financial experts because of the common example of not placing all of your investment eggs into just a single basket. If you do have all eggs in the one basket and then drop the basket along the way, then they can all break. The idea is that by placing each egg into its own individual basket, the odds of breaking all of the eggs declines significantly, even if one or several of them do get broken themselves.

Portfolios that have not engaged in diversifying might have only one or two corporations' stocks in them. This proves to be a dangerous investment strategy, since no matter how good a company looks on paper, its stock could decline to as low as zero literally over night. The past few years of the financial collapse have taught many investors the extremely painful lesson that even once blue chip financial companies' stock can decline to practically nothing as they spectacularly collapse.

Any financial expert will confidently state that portfolios made up of a dozen or two dozen varying stocks will have far less chance of plummeting. This becomes even more the case when you pick out stocks from a variety of types, industries, and market capitalization sizes of corporations. Better diversifying in stocks would include some companies that are based in other countries. Diversifying does not simply stop with stocks. It steers investors into bonds, mutual funds, and money market funds as well. Though all of these different investments diversify you, they still leave you mostly exposed to the one currency of the U.S. dollar.

More thorough diversifying will put at least a portion of your investments into assets whose values are not solely expressed in terms of only the American currency. This would include commodities, such as gold, silver, oil, and platinum in particular. Foreign currencies, such as the Euro, Pound, or Swiss Franc are another fantastic means of diversifying, and they can be acquired on the world FOREX exchange in currency accounts.

Real estate, including commercial properties, residential properties, vacation homes, or even real estate investment funds, offers another way to diversify away from U.S. dollar based financial investments such as stocks, bonds, mutual funds, and money market accounts. The strongest diversifying advice is to have at least three to seven completely different investment class vehicles, preferably one or more of which is not denominated in only U.S. dollars.

Dividend

Dividends represent portions of a company's earnings that are returned to the investors in the company's stock. These are typically paid out in cash that is either deposited into the investors' brokerage accounts or can be reinvested directly into the company's stock. As an example of a dividend, every share of Phillip Morris pays around 4.5% dividends on the stock price each year.

Investing in dividend paying stocks is a particular passive income investment strategy that is also a cash flow investment. This passive, or cash flow, income means that you collect income just from holding these stock investments. This kind of strategy entails building up a group of blue chip company stocks that pay large dividend yields which add money to your account usually four times per year, on a quarterly basis. Investors in dividends tremendously enjoy watching these routine deposits in cash arrive in either their bank account, brokerage account, or the mail.

Dividend investors who understand this type of investment are looking for a number of different elements in the stocks that they buy. Such dividend stocks should include a high dividend yield. To qualify as high yields, most value investors prefer to see ones that pay more than do the interest rate yields on U.S. Treasuries. Dividend yields can be easily determined. All that you have to do is to take the amount of the dividend and divide it by the price of the stock. So a stock that offers a $2 dividend and costs $40 is paying a five percent dividend yield.

Dividend paying stocks should also feature high dividend coverage. This coverage simply refers to the safety of a dividend, or how likely it is to be reduced or even eliminated. Companies that earn their profits from a large array of businesses are more likely to be able to continue paying their dividends than are companies that make all of their money off of a single business that could be threatened.

A more tangible way of expressing the coverage lies in how many times the dividend total dollar amount is covered by the corporation's total earnings. A company with fifty million dollars in profits that pays twenty million in dividends has its dividend covered by two and a half times. Should their profits drop by ten percent or more, they will have no trouble still paying the same dividend amount to shareholders. The dividend payout ratio is another way of measuring this. On the above example it would be forty percent. Dividend investors prefer to see no more than sixty percent of profits given out as dividends, as this could signify that the company lacks future opportunities for growth and expansion.

Qualified dividends are a third element that dividend investors are looking for in their dividend paying stocks. This simply means that stocks that are kept for less than a year do not benefit from lower tax rates on dividends. Since the government is attempting to convince you to become a longer term investor, you should take advantage of these lower tax rates by only buying stocks with qualified dividends that you have held for a full year and more.

Equifax

Equifax today is an agency that reports consumer credit within the U.S. Analysts number it among the big three American credit bureau agencies alongside rivals Trans Union and Experian. The company proves to be the oldest of the three main credit bureaus in the country as it became established back in 1899.

The firm gathers and keeps information on more than 800 million consumers and over 88 million businesses around the globe. They are headquartered in Atlanta, Georgia and remain a worldwide data services provider that has annual revenues of $2.7 billion. They have over 7,000 staff operating in 14 different countries. The company is listed on the NYSE New York Stock Exchange. One of their many divisions (Equifax Workforce Solutions) is among the 55 national contractors which the United States Department of Health and Human Services hired to help develop the federal government's HealthCare.gov website.

The original company which later became Equifax was Retail Credit Company founded in 1899. The firm rapidly expanded and already counted offices around both the United States and Canada by 1920. In the 1960s, this Retail Credit Company represented among the largest of the credit bureaus. It contained files for millions of American and Canadian citizens.

While the firm engaged in some credit reporting at the time, the main part of their business came from providing reports to the many insurance companies throughout the U.S. and Canada as consumers applied for insurance policies such as auto, life, medical, and fire insurance lines. Back in the day, every one of the significant insurance firms relied on Retail Credit Company to gather their information on health, morals, habits, finances, and the utilization of cars and vehicles. Besides this, the firm investigated various insurance claims and also gave employment reports out to companies as consumers sought new jobs. The majority of their credit reporting work at that time they delegated to a subsidiary company called Retailers Commercial Agency.

In 1975, the company changed its name to be Equifax because of image problems they had earned by keeping shady and intimate personal details on all American's lives and selling them to anyone willing to pay. It was after this that the new company Equifax expanded its operations into commercial credit reporting on firms located in the United States, the United Kingdom, and Canada. Here it engaged in competition against such firms as Experian and Dun & Bradstreet. In the 1990s, they began to phase out their insurance reporting operations and spun off their division which gathered and sold specialist credit information to insurance companies. Among this was the CLUE Comprehensive Loss Underwriting Exchange database they had developed, which they included in the Choice Point spinoff back in 1997.

Throughout the vast majority of its company history, the firm engaged mostly in the B2B sector. They sold insurance and consumer credit reports and associated analytics to businesses which operated in a variety of industries and segments. Among these were insurance firms, retailers, utilities, healthcare providers, banks, credit unions, government agencies, specialty finance companies, personal finance operations, and various other kinds of financial institutions.

Since they divested from their insurance reporting primary operation, the company sells information which includes business credit and consumer credit reports, demographic information, analytics, and software. Their credit reports offer a wide and detailed profile on the payment history and personal creditworthiness of individuals and businesses. This reveals how well these groups have honored their various financial obligations, including paying back loans and bills.

Starting in 1999, Equifax started offering its vast services into the consumer credit sector. They also began consumer operations with such important services as protection from identity theft and from credit fraud. The company along with its other two main rivals is required to offer American residents a single free credit file report once per year. The data from the U.S. Equifax credit records becomes incorporated into the Annual Credit Report.com website.

Equity

Equity represents the homeowner's total dollar amount of ownership in their property. Determining equity is a simple calculation. It is found by taking the home's assumed fair market value and subtracting out the balances of liens and debts secured by the property along with the mortgage balance that is still unpaid. As a home owner pays down the mortgage, reducing the outstanding principal balance, the equity of a home owner goes up. It similarly increases as the property gains in value. To obtain one hundred percent equity in their property, home owners have to pay down both any outstanding debts that are secured by the property and the full mortgage.

Associated with the equity value of a home is the LTV, or loan to value ratio. This loan to value ratio proves to be a means of stating the property's value as against the total dollar amount of your actual loan. The loan to value ratio is simply figured up by taking the amount of your loan and dividing it by your property value. Alternatively, you could divide the amount of your loan by the purchase price or selling price, whichever of the two is the lower amount.

An example helps to illustrate the concept. If you were to purchase a $300,000 house, you might put down a $60,000 down payment using your money. The remaining $240,000 would be covered by taking out a mortgage. Dividing the $60,000 amount by the $300,000 home value yields equity of twenty percent. If you divide the $240,000 by the $300,000 home value, then you will get the loan to value ratio that amounts to eighty percent.

Should you determine later that you will sell this house, then the equity that you have will be concretely and accurately figured up for you. This will simply prove to be the fair market value of your house minus the loan that you still owe the bank on the house. Using the example from the paragraph above, consider what would happen if you lived in and made payments on your house for five years following the purchase.

In this time frame, your monthly mortgage payments lower the balance that remains on the loan to the tune of $10,000, diminishing it from $240,000 to

$230,000. Besides this, over those five years, your home value goes up. This allows you to realize a selling price of $330,000. Since the balance that you owed is still $230,000, then your equity is simply figured by taking the $330,000 selling price and subtracting the $230,000 from it. This leaves you with a final equity value of $100,000. Once all selling costs and realty commissions are figured up and taken out, you would be able to utilize the $100,000 equity in order to invest or to put down the down payment on the next house that you purchase.

Naturally, this home value can cut both ways. Should the value on the home drop from $300,00 to $250,000 in the time that you own it, then your remaining equity would be only $50,000, less than the original $60,000 that you put into it upfront.

Escrow

Escrow is a concept that relates to a sum of money that is kept by an uninvolved third party for the two parties involved in a given transaction. In the U.S., this escrow is most commonly involved where real estate mortgages are concerned. Here is it utilized for the payment of insurance and property tax during the mortgage's life.

When you place your money into such an escrow account, an escrow agent who is a neutral third party holds it. This agent works on behalf of both the borrower and home lender. The escrow agent's job in the transaction is to act as the principal parties instruct him or her. As all transaction terms are fulfilled, the money is then released. These escrow accounts may be a part of transactions ranging from small purchases affected on online auction sites to building projects that total in the multiple millions of dollars.

Escrow is utilized in these property transactions when it is time for your mortgage to close. At this point, the borrower's lender will commonly insist that you establish an escrow account for paying for both home owner's insurance and property taxes. You are required to make a first deposit to the account. After this, you make payments into the account each month. Typically, these are simply a part of your monthly mortgage payments. When it is time for your insurance premiums and taxes to be paid, your escrow agent then releases the funds.

The concept behind this escrow is to give your lender peace of mind and protection that your insurance and taxes are both paid in a timely manner. Should you not pay your property taxes, the city might place a lien on this house, making it hard for the bank to sell it if they needed to. Similarly, if a fire burned down the house and the insurance premiums had not been paid, the bank would not have any underlying collateral for the mortgage anymore.

You the borrower also benefit from this escrow account. It allows you to stretch out your taxes and insurance costs over the course of the entire year's twelve payments. As an example, your annual property taxes might prove to be $3,000, with a yearly insurance cost of $600. This would mean that when spread out over twelve even payments, the escrow costs would amount to only $300 each month.

The nice thing about escrow accounts and payments is that they come with an included safeguard built in. Should you miss a single payment, then the responsible lender is still capable of paying the accounts in a timely manner. The U.S. Federal law actually stops these lenders from storing up in excess of two months' worth of payments in escrow. As insurance and tax amounts will vary a little from one year to the next, the lender will have to examine and make adjustments to your annual escrow payments.

Expenses

Expenses refer to costs that business undergo in order to conduct their daily business operations, expand and grow their business, and acquire additional assets, property and factories. Firms are capable of investing their cash into a few different kinds of investments. They might buy a new building or some real estate. They could similarly purchase office or computer equipment for their premises. They might update older technology for the firm or aging machinery for production so that the business gains a higher level of productivity. These companies might also acquire vehicles for their traveling staff, such as executives, sales people, or for their delivery personnel. Any of these various types of investments would be for capital assets, which would make them capital expenses (sometimes also called expenditures).

Such expenses represent payments that a firm makes to acquire or increase the performance of longer-term capital assets such as equipment, factories, and buildings. These are generally expensive and substantial purchases which companies pursue for a corporate investment. Another way of thinking about this is that such capital expenses increase the overall business value. In consequence, as the asset values gain, so too does the net worth of the owner or stake holders. Yet at the same time the expenses incurred in acquiring the asset will similarly increase the liability of the owners.

Another expense that businesses realize analysts call depreciation. This simply means that assets decline naturally in value with time. It diminishes the company's value as it inevitably occurs. Such costs of capital expenses thus can be depreciated or capitalized throughout a given amount of time. This time equates to what the business world refers to as the useful life of the asset in question.

It always helps to consider an example of difficult concepts like these. When companies acquire equipment in the office for $20,000, they can depreciate this expense amount over a period of five years. It means that they will be allowed to take their depreciation of capital expense to the tune of $4,000 per year. Sometimes, this depreciation can be accelerated so that businesses realize the expense benefits quicker. There are also accountants who choose to include such intangible assets as copyrights, trademarks, and patents in the capital expenses category. Such assets become amortized, which is not unlike the process of depreciation in many ways.

It follows that companies should be able to expense the costs to keep a given capital asset up, in service, and working properly and efficiently. While this surmise is true, it cannot be done under the capital expense categories. Instead, they are treated as operating expenses in many cases. Yet with repairing equipment, this would likely increase its value. In that instance, this would represent a capital expense. This is why tax professionals have to help firms with figuring up the appropriate categories and depreciating.

Some other types of assets cannot be depreciated at all. Land is one of these. Because real estate does not lose value, the IRS considers that it possesses an indefinite value. This means firms may not depreciate real estate like they can with capital expense and operating costs.

When all else is equal, companies would rather obtain their tax deductions for asset purchases sooner rather than later. Yet the Internal Revenue Service has something to say on the subject. They maintain the rigorous rules on what may or may not be expensed out immediately. Startup costs are a good example of this. They will certainly boost the firm's value but they are spent upfront. The IRS permits just a certain quantity of such startup costs to be expensed out during the first year of business. The rest of these have to be amortized. In 2015, the government passed new legislation that permitted for more liberal benefits of corporate depreciation for those companies that buy capital assets.

Experian

Experian is one of the three main credit reporting bureaus in the United States. As such it maintains a credit report, history, and FICO score on all adult Americans. The company does so much more than this most commonly understood function.

The company is also an international leader for global business and consumer credit reporting as well as marketing services. Experian is headquartered in Dublin, Ireland and is based on the London Stock Exchange where it is a member of Britain's FTSE 100 stock index. The company has customers in over 80 countries of the world and maintains offices and employees in 37 countries. Besides its Dublin base, Experian has operations headquarters found in Nottingham in the United Kingdom, California in the United States, and Sao Paulo in Brazil.

Experian serves as the corporate leader in global information services. The company received the 2015 honor of "World's Most Innovative Companies" from Forbes magazine for being among the leaders in driving improvements and change.

They deliver analytical tools and data to their clients found all over the world. The company helps businesses to prevent fraud, to manage their credit risk, to automate functions of decision making, and to specifically target marketing offers.

Experian also assists individuals with information and security needs. They aid individuals in checking out their credit reports and credit scores through copies that they can purchase and download directly over the Internet. They help people to safeguard themselves against the very real dangers of identity theft with credit report monitoring services. The company also provides a great source of information for education that is both hands on and interactive. This education helps both marketing personnel and credit professionals along with individual consumers.

Experian prides itself on its analytic and data services. They are in the business of assisting businesses and individuals with managing, protecting, and optimally using their data. They offer a number of different services to help people to do this effectively.

Their Experian Credit Tracker product gives consumers their FICO score, Experian credit report, and a credit monitoring service that comes with fraud alerts. They also staff a dedicated support team for fraud resolution when individuals become victims of identity theft. Help with identity theft or credit fraud is an area that is critical to consumers when they become victims.

Consumers can also choose from their higher level Experian Protect My ID service. This gives individuals an Experian credit report, 3 bureau credit monitoring services and alerts, daily checking of ID via Internet scanning, and access to their dedicated support for fraud resolution.

Experian provides a higher level view of individuals' credit reports and scores also. Their 3 Bureau Credit Report and FICO Scores service delivers copies of the person's credit report and FICO score for Experian, TransUnion, and Equifax. They also sell just their own credit report and FICO score for a lower price.

Experian offers even more services to its big business customers. Among their business product offerings are customer acquisition, customer management, fraud management, risk management, debt recovery, consulting services, regulatory compliance, and thought leadership. In customer acquisition, the company offers direct mail tools and big data analytics.

For risk management they verify applicants' identities and backgrounds. Experian can manage data breaches and prevent money laundering as part of their fraud management offerings. Debt recovery services include locating debtors and managing collection efforts. Among their consulting services are strategy, product, and fraud consulting areas.

Small business customers also have a variety of services offered to them by Experian. These include help with business and consumer credit, marketing and managing the business, and collecting debt.

Fannie Mae

Fannie Mae is the acronym for the FNMA Federal National Mortgage Association. This entity is a GSE Government Sponsored Enterprise along with brother organization Freddie Mac. It became a publicly traded company in 1968. This home lending giant proves to be the largest mortgage financing provider anywhere in the United States. As such, it funds significantly more mortgages than any competing company or entity. It ensures that homebuyers, homeowners, and renters around the U.S. all can obtain financing options which they can afford.

As the GSE became established in 1938, it has provided funding for the housing market of the country for over 75 years. Franklin D. Roosevelt's New Deal established the company in the midst of the Great Depression. This is why the mission of the company is to aid individuals in purchasing, renting, or refinancing a home whether economic times in the country are good or bad.

The company's explicit purpose is to boost the size of the secondary mortgage market. They do this when they securitize mortgages and package them into MBS mortgage backed securities. This process returns the mortgage loaned money to lenders who are then able to reinvest this money into additional lending. It also acts to grow the numbers of lending institutions who are issuing mortgages. This ensures that there are more than just savings and loan associations making local loans for housing.

The model worked well until between 2003 and 2004. At this point the subprime mortgages crisis started. It began when the mortgage market turned away from the GSEs like Freddie Mac and Fannie Mae and began to migrate rapidly to unregulated MBS Mortgage Backed Securities that major investment banks put together. This shift to private MBSs caused the GSEs to lose their control over and ability to monitor mortgages in the country.

Increased competition between the investment banks and the GSEs reduced the power and market share of the government mortgage backers further and boosted the mortgage lenders at their expense. This radical change in the way mortgages were overseen and made caused the underwriting standards for mortgages to dangerously decline. It turned out to be one of the major reasons for the ensuing mortgage and financial crises.

The situation became so severe at Fannie Mae by 2008 that the FHFA Federal Housing Finance Agency had to get directly involved. FHFA Director James Lockhart on September 7, 2008 placed both this organization and Freddie Mac under FHFA conservatorship. This proved to be among the most dramatic and far reaching government involvements in free enterprise financial markets for literally decades.

Among Lockhart's first actions, he fired both companies' boards of directors and CEOs. He then made the companies issue a new class of common stock warrants and senior preferred stock to Treasury for 79.9% of both GSEs. Those who had been holding either preferred or common stock in either entity before the conservatorship began saw the value of their shares massively decrease. All prior shares' dividends became suspended to try to hold up the mortgage backed securities' and company debt values. FHFA pledged that it had no intentions of liquidating the GSEs.

Since 2009, Fannie Mae has made great strides in its business of helping make housing work better for individuals and families. They have injected trillions of dollars into the mortgage markets in lending liquidity. This has gone a long way to helping the housing markets and overall economy to recover.

The company has also gone back to high quality eligibility and underwriting standards. In the first quarter of 2016, they have extended $115 billion in mortgage credit that has allowed for 210,000 homes to be purchased and 256,000 mortgages to be refinanced. They also financed the construction of 161,000 multifamily rental units.

Federal Reserve

The Federal Reserve, also known as the Fed, or the Federal Reserve Board, proves to be the United States' central banking system. This central bank came about in 1913 as a result of Congress passing the Federal Reserve Act. Congress created the organization because of a number of serious financial panics that culminated in the severe panic of 1907.

With time, the Federal Reserve's roles and areas of responsibility have grown as the organization has expanded. Economic events such as the Great Depression have only served to encourage this.

The Federal Reserve today counts among its duties many responsibilities. Among these are regulating and overseeing the country's banks, managing the country's monetary policy and supply, assuring the financial systems' continuance and stability, and offering a variety of financial services to depositing banks, foreign central banks, and the United States government.

The Federal Reserve's structure is made up of a number of different components. Among these are the Federal Reserve Board of Governors, all of whom are appointed by the President. The Federal Open Market Committee, also known by its acronym of FOMC, sets the monetary policy, like the interest rates, for the nation. There are also Federal Reserve Banks, which are twelve regional institutions that are found in the biggest area cities around America. They offer physical currency to member banks when demand proves to be unusually high. Several councils that advise it are a part of The Federal Reserve, as are technically the member banks throughout the country.

The FOMC component of the Federal Reserve is actually comprised of all of these seven Board of Governors members along with the presidents of the twelve regional banks. Only five of these presidents are voting members at a time. Together, they review the state of the U.S. national economy in order to determine what fiscal policies need to be pursued. When the economic growth is slowing, or a recession is occurring, they cut the national interest rates. When inflation is appearing or the economy is overheating, they raise these interest rates.

The Federal Reserve proves to be a unique entity among the major central banks. This is because it divides up the various responsibilities into some public and some private parts of the institution. The Federal Reserve furthermore serves to create the currency used for the country, the U.S. dollar. The fact that it is both a public and private institution, with so many varied and vast powers, makes it one of a kind.

Because the U.S. dollar is still the reserve currency of the world, the Federal Reserve's powers are far greater than simply managing the U.S. economy. In actual practice, they also are the custodians and managers of the world's reserve currency. This gives them considerable power and influence throughout the entire world economy, since they are able to create not only dollars for the U.S. economy, but also for other central banks use in foreign countries. As a result of this, more than half of the physically printed U.S. dollars are found outside of the United States.

Fiat Money

Fiat Money proves to be money that has no real intrinsic, or actual, value. It instead derives its worth from governments accepting it as legal tender. The concept of fiat money on a large scale is a relatively new one. Throughout practically all of history, the majority of currencies around the world derived their value from silver or gold. Fiat money is instead entirely based on trust and faith in the issuing monetary authority.

The problem with fiat money lies in the ability of the governments to inflate its value away. They can do this by over printing it. Since fiat currencies are not restricted by a requirement of hard reserve assets, they can be created in any quantity that the issuing government desires. As the supply continues to rise while the demand remains constant, its purchasing power will fall. When the supply is drastically increased, then hyperinflation will result. Fiat money that falls by hundreds of percent in value is deemed to be a victim of hyperinflation.

The other disadvantage is that only peoples' trust in it ultimately gives it practical value. It suffers from inflation and finally hyperinflation, then the confidence in it becomes shaken. Fiat money that lacks the confidence of its citizens will finally collapse in value and then no longer be of any trading use for daily transactions. When it fails, people either return to barter systems, or the government establishes a currency based on hard assets once again.

The history of money has proven on a number of occasions that governments debase currency to the point of fiat money when it suits them. They do this because it allows them to print as much as they need to pay for things. While this creates inflation for their citizens, it gives the money issuing government the ability to repay their debts with cheaper fiat money. Finally, as a society has had enough of the devalued money and currency instability, they force the government to return to asset backed money. This has happened before, and some monetary experts say that you are starting to see this happen again nowadays.

FICO Score

FICO Score refers to the overwhelmingly most popular and heavily utilized credit score in the United States. The company which created, owns, and manages it to this day is Fair Isaac Corporation. Financial institutions that loan out money employ this FICO score for an individual to assess any credit risk and decide whether or not they will offer the person credit. Sometimes they also consider specific information on the credit report of the borrower, but this is increasingly uncommon.

The reason for this is that the FICO score contemplates a well-rounded set of risk parameters for the would-be borrowers. These five areas it considers and draws upon to issue a credit score for credit worthiness include the individual's payment history, present amount of debts, types of credit utilized, amount of credit history, and new credit inquiries and issued accounts.

Ninety percent of financial institutions in the United States that offer loans rely on the FICO score for assessing the creditworthiness of an individual. These scores vary from as low as 300 to as high as 850. Generally speaking, scores over 650 represent desirable credit history. Individuals who boast less than 620 conversely typically find it hard to get decent financing offers approved at reasonable interest rates. Financial institutions claim that they also consider various other details besides FICO scores. These include history of time at a job, applicant's income, and the kind of credit they are seeking.

It is interesting and illuminating to understand how the three main credit bureaus calculate this FICO Score. Fair Isaac Corporation has its proprietary model in which they weigh all categories differently for every individual. This makes it more difficult to say with certainty what percentages in each of the five categories they consider.

Yet generally speaking, payment history represents 35 percent of the total. Amount owed on accounts comprises 30 percent generally. Amount of years of credit history equals approximately 15 percent. Credit mix equates to around 10 percent. New credit inquiries and accounts represent about 10 percent.

Payment history is the simple answer to the question, "does the individual borrower pay the accounts in a timely fashion?" Thanks to the exhaustive nature of credit history, the bureaus clearly demonstrate the payments which have been made for every single line of credit. The reports make special note if any of the payments came in 30, 60, 90, 120, or still more days later than due.

Amounts owed on accounts pertains to the dollar amounts individuals owe on their various accounts as a percentage of the total available credit. This does not mean that possessing a great amount of debt ruins a credit score. What the Fair Isaac Company is considering is the ratio of amount owed to amount available. A clear example shows that when Ringo owed $100,000 yet was not near his limits on any of the accounts, he had a higher credit score than George who only owed $25,000 yet had nearly maxed out his credit card accounts.

Credit history length is a complex category. FICO considers the age of the oldest account as well as the age of the most recent one. They then compile the average account age and come up with a value for this category. Those with shorter credit histories can still get a good credit score.

Credit mix pertains to the variety in types of credit accounts. Higher category credit scores go to those people who have a strong and varied mix of credit cards, retail accounts, and installment loans like mortgages, vehicle loans, and signature loans.

Finally, the Fair Isaac Company does not like recently opened accounts in much of any quantity. When borrowers take out a range of new credit lines and accounts in only a brief amount of time, this tells them that the person is becoming a credit risk and thus decreases the total FICO score.

Financial Statement

Financial statements are official records of a business' or personal financial activity. With businesses, financial statements present any and all pertinent financial activity as usable information. They do this in a clear, organized, and simple to comprehend way.

Financial statements are commonly comprised of four different types of financial accounts that come with an analysis and discussion provided by the company's management. The Balance sheet is the first of these. It is known by several other names, including statement of financial condition, or statement of financial position. The balance sheet details will outline a corporation's ownership equity, liabilities, and assets on a particular date. This will give a good picture of the general strength and position of the company.

Financial statements similarly include income statements. These can also be called Profit and Loss statements too. They outline numerous important pieces of company information, such as corporate expenses, income, and profits made in a certain time period. This statement explains all of the relevant financial details to the business' operation. Sales and all associated expenses are included under this category. This section of the financial statement proves to be the nuts and bolts of the whole document. It provides a snap shot of the company's ability to generate sales and turn profits.

A statement of cash flow is also a part of a complete financial statement. As its name implies, this section will share all of the details regarding the company's activities pertaining to cash flow. The most important ones that will be outlined include operating cash flow, financing, and investing endeavors.

The last element of a financial statement includes the statement of retained earnings. This section of the document makes good on its name to detail any changes to a corporation's actual retained earnings for the period that is being reported. These four sections of a financial statement are all combined together to make the consolidated financial statement, once they are combined with the analysis and discussion of management.

With large multinational types of corporations, such financial statements are typically large and complicated, making them challenging to read and understand. To assist with readability, they may also come with a group of notes for the financial statement that also covers management's analysis and discussion. Such notes will go through all items listed on the four parts of the financial statement in more thorough detail. For many companies, these notes for financial statements have come to be deemed a critical component of good and complete financial statements.

Financial statements are used by several different groups of people who are looking at a company. Investors use them in order to determine if the company and its stocks or bonds make a sound investment with a chance of providing good returns on investments and profits in exchange for limited risks. Banks utilize these financial statements to decide if a company is a good credit risk for their loan dollars. Institutions and other groups that may be considering a cash infusion or buyout of the company use such financial statements to decide if the company is a viable investment or acquisition target.

Foreclosure

Foreclosures represent houses or commercial properties that have been seized by a bank or other mortgage lender. These properties are then sold to recoup mortgage loan losses after an owner and borrower has not made the payments as promised in the mortgage agreement.

Foreclosure is also the legal procedure in which the lender gets a court order for the termination of the mortgagor's right of redemption. This is the case since most lenders have security interests in the house from the borrower. The borrower will secure the mortgage using the house as the collateral.

Borrowers fall into home foreclosure for several reasons, most of which could not be predicted in advance. Owner might have been let go from their job or forced to take a job transfer to another state. They might have suffered from medical problems that prevented them from working. They might have gone through a divorce and split up assets. They could have been overwhelmed by too many bills. Whatever the reason, they are no longer able to make their promised monthly mortgage payments.

Foreclosures represent potential opportunities for investors. They may be purchased directly with a seller in advance of a bank completing foreclosure proceedings. Many investors who concentrate on foreclosures prefer to deal with the owners directly. They have to be aware of many laws pertaining to foreclosures, which are different in every state. For example, while in some states home owners can stay in their properties for a full year after defaulting on payments, while in others, they have fewer than four months in advance of the trustee sale.

Practically all states also allow a redemption period for the delinquent homeowner. This simply means that a seller possesses an irrevocable ability to catch up on back payments and interest in order to retain ownership of the house. The owner will likely be required to pay any foreclosure costs experienced by the bank up to that point.

Another means of purchasing a foreclosure home is to buy it at the Trustee's Sale. When this means is pursued, it is better to bid on a house that allows you to look it over in advance of putting up an offer. This is helpful so that you can determine how many repairs will be needed to make it salable and even possibly habitable. It is also worth knowing if the occupants are still living in the house and will have to be forcefully evicted. The process of going through an eviction can be both expensive and time consuming.

Many Trustee Sales will have certain rules in common that have to be followed for a foreclosure house to be purchased. They may demand sealed bids. They could require you to demonstrate your proof of financial qualifications. They might similarly insist on you putting up a significant earnest money deposit. Many of them will state that the property is being purchased in its present condition, or as is.

Franchise

A franchise can be defined in many ways. The definition from the International Franchise Association describes franchising as a means to expand a business so that goods and services can be distributed more effectively via a licensing relationship. The word itself legally means a specific kind of license. Ultimately, franchising refers to the personal relationship which a franchisor maintains with its franchisees.

In this arrangement, the franchisor licenses out its trade name as well as its operating methods, or systematic way of doing business, to a particular franchisee. In exchange for this arrangement, the franchisee pledges to run the business as per the terms of this license. The operating method here refers to the franchisor's system and way of doing business.

Franchisors guarantee their franchisees will have their support and help. They also maintain a certain level of control over specific parts of the franchisee business. This is critical for the franchise owner to safeguard its intellectual property rights as well as to be certain that the franchisee keeps to the guidelines of the brand itself. The quid pro quo of this is that the franchisee typically delivers a one time start up fee (known as the franchise fee) to the franchisor. The franchisees also pay a royalty fee to the franchisor, which is periodic and continuous. This enables the franchisee to utilize the franchisor's operating system and trade name.

The franchisor itself carries little responsibility for involvement in the daily management of the business of the franchisee. This is because franchisees exist as independent operators. Neither are they joint employers with their franchisors. This gives the franchisees a free hand in hiring employees, paying them according to their wishes, scheduling their shifts as they see fit, arranging their employment rules and practices, and even disciplining their own employees, all without requiring any approval from their franchisor. However, the uniforms which the employees wear will be stipulated by the brand and operating system of the franchisor.

Franchising is about a contractually defined relationship between the two parties. The franchisees and franchisor will share the brand in common. Despite this, both are distinctly separate businesses in both real terms and legally. The role of the franchisor is simply to build up its business and brand as part of supporting the various franchisees. The part which the franchisees play is to operate and manage their own business according to the specific terms of the franchise agreements.

It is interesting that definitions of franchises range from one state to the next according to the various laws which different states enforce. Some states include among the various elements of franchising the responsibilities of the franchisor to deliver a marketing plan to its franchisees. Others insist that the franchisor maintain an interested community of the business jointly with the franchisee.

Business Format Franchises are the most readily recognizable types of these arrangements for the everyday individual. These relationships typically cover the whole of the business and its format, not only the products, services, and trade name of the franchisor in question. In this common type, franchisors are expected to give their franchisees training, operating manuals, standards for the brand, a marketing plan and strategy to carry it out, quality control monitoring, and more.

Examples of the idea make these distinctions clear. Pizza Hut does not license out pizzas or breadsticks. Burger King does not license out hamburgers or chicken sandwiches. The two mega franchise operations instead license out components of their intellectual property. In this case it includes both their business systems and their trade marks, or their ways of producing these food items and company-described premises and atmosphere.

The history of these and other brands demonstrates that both services and products have changed significantly over the decades. Among the various advantages to these types of business format franchises and their arrangements is that they have the flexibility to do so effectively.

Today there exist numerous kinds of franchises throughout a constantly expanding array of industries and market segments in not only the United States and Canada but around the globe. Estimates state that more than 120 separate industries utilize the concept and practices of franchising now. The greatest share of franchising by far is still the food and restaurants businesses. Nowadays even medical services and home based health care rely on franchising though.

Freddie Mac

Freddie Mac is a semi-private company that Congress chartered in 1970. They created the entity to offer stability, liquidity, and affordable prices for the country and its housing markets. They have grown to be responsible for the home purchases of one out of four buyers.

Besides this the company is also among the biggest financing sources for multifamily housing in the nation. From 2009 to 2016, the company has dispersed mortgage market funding that amounts to over $2.5 trillion. This has enabled in excess of 13 million American families to refinance, purchase, or rent a home in that time frame.

In 1970 Congress was seeking to stabilize the mortgage markets of the country. They wanted to grow and improve opportunities for rental housing that was affordable and for home buying. Because of this, Freddie Mac's mission has always been to bring stability, liquidity, and affordability to the national housing market in the United States. They do this in a variety of ways. The company helps the secondary mortgage market. They buy both mortgage securities and mortgage loans outright as investments. They then package and sell these as guaranteed mortgage securities known as PCs. In this secondary market, there are entities which buy and sell mortgages as complete loans or as mortgage securities. Freddie Mac never makes loans to home owners directly themselves.

Because of the collapse of the mortgage backed securities markets in 2007 and 2008 and its impact on their finances, the company is now being run under conservatorship. The FHFA Federal Housing Finance Agency oversees their business to make sure loans are carefully scrutinized and securitized. They want to avoid the mistakes of the financial crisis becoming repeated here.

Freddie Mac operates in three main business areas to ensure that a continuous supply of mortgage funding goes through to the housing markets in the country. They make rental housing and home buying more affordable through their single family credit guarantee business, their multifamily business, and their investment business. They utilize all three of these to promote financing for affordable housing.

The single family line is essentially a recycling operation. They work with securitizing mortgages so that the entity is able to provide funding to millions of different home loans annually. This securitization proves to be the means where they buy up different loans lenders have made and then package these up into various mortgage securities. They then sell these on the worldwide capital markets. The money from the sale of these securities they next funnel back to the lenders. In this way home loan operations have sufficient mortgage money for lending.

The company is also interested in supporting renters as well. This is the role of their multifamily business. In this line, the outfit cooperates with a group of lenders to help finance the construction of various apartment buildings throughout the United States. The lenders make the loans and Freddie Mac buys them to package and resell. This way the lenders receive back the proceeds so they can issue more loans. This is a critical line as multifamily loans prove to be a few million dollars each and require unique underwriting from one property to the next.

Their investment business actually purchases some of their own mortgage backed securities which they and other financial entities like Fannie Mae guarantee. This portfolio further invests into individual loans which they guarantee but choose not to securitize. By bidding on some of their own securities, the investment business and portfolio serves the markets. It gives these mortgage backed securities greater liquidity and offers more funding for mortgages. They do this by issuing their own debt which creates net income for the company after they pay their interest to the bond holders.

Gross Income

Gross income can be several different things in the United States. In tax law for business, gross income signifies all proceeds realized from every source minus the cost of goods that have been sold. It is also used for individuals and pertains to all income earned from any and every kind of source.

As such, it is not simply cash that has been realized, but it can also be income received in kind, as property, or as services. For a taxpayer, gross income is commonly believed to be all of the monies and values received. Although most income is tallied into this figure, a few kinds of income are excluded deliberately.

For companies, individuals, trusts, estates, and others, gross income is necessary for figuring up the mandatory income taxes within the United States. Taxes are figured up using a taxable income number that starts with gross income and then subtracts permissible tax deductions. Taxes are then calculated based on the resulting taxable income.

Many different types of income are considered to be a part of the gross income category. Wages are the earnings for work performed payable as tips, salaries, and related income. Income made as a result of such personal service is always tallied up in a person's gross income. Gross profits made from selling an inventory of products are also considered gross income. Gross profits result from sales prices of items minus the cost of the goods actually sold.

All interest received is also considered to be a part of gross income. Dividends, along with distributions of capital gains from companies or mutual funds are similarly a part of gross income. Gains on property that has been disposed of are also tallied into the gross income total after the extra proceeds beyond the adjusted cost in the property is determined. Also included are royalties and rents from intangible and tangible items.

A number of other non traditional types of income are also considered to be a part of this. Pensions, income from life insurance, and annuities income are counted. So are alimony, child support, and other maintenance payments. Shares of partnership income that are distributed fall under this category. Even the proceeds from national and state tax refunds are considered to be gross income.

The Internal Revenue Service claims that such gross income includes all forms of income from any source of which they are derived. As such, gross income can result from any gains having to do with labor, capital, the two together, or profits having to do with the sale of anything or a capital asset. A notable exception to gross income includes gifts and inheritances. While these could be taxed under the category of estate taxes or gift taxes, they are not deemed by the IRS to be a part of gross income.

Gross Margin

Gross Margin is also known as gross profit margin. This concept represents a business formula that companies compute. It is best expressed as the firm's total revenue less its cots of goods sold which is then divided by the total revenue. This provides the answer as a percentage. In other words, Gross Margins are the percentage of revenues the corporations keep after paying their direct expenses of creating both their services and goods. Higher percentages mean a company keeps a larger amount of every dollar worth of sales. This greater amount of retained income provides it with more money for servicing debt, making new investments, retained earnings, and paying out dividends to shareholders.

Gross margin equates to the amount from every sales dollar that the firm is able to keep for their gross profits. Consider a concrete and tangible real world example to better understand this idea. If HSBC Bank has a gross margin in a quarter of 30 percent, then this means it keeps 30 cents from every dollar in revenue it creates. The other 70 cents would go into the Cost of Goods Sold (COGS) category. Since all of the bank's COGS are already considered, the other 30 cents per dollar in revenue may be applied to general overhead, paying down any debt, expenses on interest, and shareholder dividend distributions.

Corporations utilize this gross margin in order to ascertain how their costs of production are measuring up against their revenues. When a corporation's gross margin is declining, it will try to find ways to reduce its costs of suppliers and labor costs. The supplier costs can be slashed by finding alternative suppliers who will supply the goods at lower prices. The other solution is to try to raise the prices on the company goods and services so as to increase the value of the corporate sales revenues.

Another effective use of gross margins lies in predicting the amount of money which they will retain towards general operating costs. Companies with 45 percent gross margins know they will have to work with 45 cents on each dollar of revenue they collect in order cover their remaining administrative and operating costs. The measure also allows for firms to measure up their efficiency as a company. Investors and analysts are able to compare and contrast two or more corporations of varying sizes against one another with the metric as well.

Gross margin should never be erroneously confused with net profit margin. Gross margin simply considers the connection between the cost of goods sold and the sales revenue. On the other hand, net profit margin covers every expense a corporation has. Calculating up the net profit margins requires firms to start with their revenues and subtract out their cost of goods sold and other expenses. This includes sales rep wages, distribution of product costs, taxes, and various operating costs.

Another way of looking at the differences between the two related but still different concepts is that the gross profit margin allows firms to determine the level of their manufacturing operations' profitability. Alternatively the net profit margin assists firms in considering their level of all around profitability.

Consider another example for calculating up gross profit margin. If a company brings in two million dollars in sales revenue, it might spend $800,000 on its labor expenses and another $200,000 on the manufacturing inputs. Once these costs of goods sold of one million dollars are subtracted out, a full million dollars remains in total gross profits. When individuals take the gross profits and divide it by the total revenue, the result is 0.5. Turned into a percentage, this equals a gross profit margin of 50 percent.

Hedging

In the world of finance, hedging is the act of putting together a hedge. Hedging involves building up a position in one market whose goal is try to counteract risk from changes in price in another market's position that is the opposite. The ultimate goal is to diminish or eliminate the business or person's possibilities of risk that they wish to avoid. A number of specific vehicles exist to help with hedging. These typically include forward contracts, swaps, insurance policies, options, derivatives, and products sold over the counter. Futures contracts prove to be the most popular version of hedging instruments.

In the 1800's, futures markets open to the public came into existence. These were set up to permit a standardized form of effective, viable, and open hedging of commodity prices in agriculture. In the intervening century, these have grown to include all manners of futures contracts that allow individuals and businesses to hedge precious metals, energy, changes in interest rates, and movements in foreign currencies.

There are countless examples of individuals who might be interested in hedging. Commercial farmers are common types of people who practice hedging. Prices for agricultural crops like wheat change all the time as the demand and supply for them fluctuates. Sometimes these price changes are significant in one direction or the other. With the present prices and crop predictions at harvest time, a commercial farmer might determine that planting wheat for the season is smart.

The problem that he encounters is that these predicted prices are simply forecasts. After the farmer plants his wheat crop, he has tied himself to it for the whole growing season. Should the real price of wheat soar in between the time that the farmer plants and harvests his crop then he might make a great amount of money that he did not count on, yet should the real price decline by the time the harvest is in then the farmer might be ruined completely.

To remove the risk from his wheat crop equation, the farmer can set up a hedge. He does this hedging by selling a certain quantity of futures contracts for wheat. These should be sold at an amount equal to the wheat crop size that he expects when he plants it. In such a way, the commercial farmer fixes his price of wheat at planting time. His hedging contract proves to be a pledge to furnish a particular quantity of wheat bushels to a certain place on a fixed date in time at a guaranteed price. Now the farmer is hedged against changes in the prices of wheat. He does not have to worry anymore about the wheat prices and whether they are falling or rising, since he has been promised a fixed price in his hedging wheat futures contract. The possibility of him being totally ruined by falling wheat prices is completely removed from the realm of possibility. At the same time, he has lost the opportunity of realizing extra money as a result of rising wheat prices when harvest time arrives. These are the upsides and the downsides to hedging; both the positives and the negatives of uncertainty are eliminated.

Holdings

Holdings refer to the asset contents in a given portfolio which an entity or individual possesses. Pension funds and mutual funds are good examples of organizations that have holdings. These positions can include all sorts of different investment assets and classes. Among these are stocks, mutual funds, bonds, futures, options, ETF exchange traded funds, and private equity assets.

It is both the kinds and amounts of such holdings in any portfolios that determine how well-diversified the portfolio actually proves to be. Well-diversified portfolios often include various sectors of stocks, bonds from a range of maturities and companies, and a variety of other investments that do not correlate with either stocks or bonds. Alternatively, only a few positions in several stocks that come from only one sector would be indicative of poorly diversified portfolios.

It is actually the mix and amount of various asset classes in any portfolio that will substantially determine what its total rate of return will be. The biggest positions will exert a larger impact on the return of a portfolio than marginal or tinier holdings in such a portfolio will. Many investors make it a practice to closely scrutinize the lists of positions which the world's most successful money managers maintain in an effort to follow their trades.

Such investors try to imitate the trading prowess of these superior results money managers in a variety of ways. It might be the manager has purchased stocks, in which case the imitating investors will try to stake out a similar company position. If these managers sell out of a stake, the investors will similarly sell off their assets in the company. The problem with such a follower strategy is that there is often substantial lag time between that point where the money managers make their moves and when this information becomes public domain knowledge.

There is another variation on the idea of mutual funds, hedge funds, and pension funds. This is the concept of holding companies. Such organizations are groups where the investors organize their positions and assets as an LLC Limited Liability Company. The reasons for this are varied. It might be they wish to decrease their own risk exposure, pool their investment dollars with fellow investors, and/or reduce their taxes as much as possible. Such companies rarely operate their own businesses directly. Instead, they are generally only a vehicle utilized to own various investments and companies.

Probably the best-known example of such an LLC company is the internationally followed Berkshire Hathaway, Inc. This Warren Buffet-dominated Omaha, Nebraska- based corporation originally began as a clothing textiles' manufacturing firm. Over the last numbers of decades, the corporation has solely existed as Warren Buffet's personal vehicle to buy out, maintain, and sell out his numerous and wide-ranging investments in various companies. Among the greatest and most significant positions which Berkshire owns are large stakes in the Coca-Cola Company, Dairy Queen Inc, and their wholly controlled subsidiary GEICO Government Employees Insurance Company.

The simplest way to envision these holdings is to mentally picture a large bucket, which represents the mutual fund. Every rock within the bucket stands for an individual bond or stock position. When analysts add up all of the rocks (as stocks or bonds), this equals the aggregate numbers of all holdings.

Figuring out the best mix of these holdings is the challenge that mutual funds, pension funds, and hedge funds all grapple with on a regular basis. It all comes down to the type of fund which they represent. Those bond funds or index funds would anticipate having many positions. This could mean from hundreds to thousands of different bonds and stocks. With the majority of other funds, too many or too few positions is risky and dangerous. Those funds that hold merely 30 positions would be subject to extreme volatility and single stock risks. If they had 500 to 600 different stocks or bonds then the fund would be as large as many indices like the S&P 500.

Home Equity

Home Equity refers to those assets which result from the home owner's stake in the house itself. Calculating up the equity of the home is not difficult. One simply takes any remaining loan balances and subtracts them off of the market value of the property. It is very possible for the equity in a home to grow with time, in particular when the value of the property rises and also as the balance of the loan becomes gradually paid down over time.

An easier way to think of this home equity is as the part of the property which the home owner actually owns. The lender is always the interest holder in a given property that includes a mortgage secured by the home. This is the case all the way up to the point where the home owner pays off completely the mortgage loan balance. It is no exaggeration to state that the equity in a home is commonly the most valuable asset for most home buyers. Equity in a home allows for a home owner to take out a second mortgage at later points in the life of the mortgage loan.

It is always helpful to look at a real-world example to better understand difficult and challenging concepts such as this one. If a home buyer obtained a house for $250,000 and dutifully made a full 20 percent down payment, then he would likely obtain a $200,000 mortgage loan to pay the remaining balance on the house. The home equity at this initial point would equate to the down payment of $50,000. The home's value is $250,000, but the buyer only contributed $50,000 as an upfront down payment towards the purchase price.

In the unlikely event that the value of the home doubled, it would then be worth $500,000. Yet despite this windfall increase in value, the mortgage is still only $200,000. This would mean that the home equity increased to a massive $300,000. The equity stake then would have risen to 60 percent. Figuring this up is simply a function of dividing the balance of the loan by the market value to subtract the end result from one. Then the person must convert the resulting decimal into a percentage. While the balance on the mortgage has not grown, the equity in the home has massively increased.

There are several ways that a home owner might increase the equity within his home. The simplest way is to pay down the loan balance at a faster rate than only the monthly mortgage payment amounts. Slowly over time, these monthly payments will go more and more towards the principal repayment. It means that all else being equal, a person builds up the equity in the home at a rate that increases gradually every year. By making extra payments each month, which all accrue against the principal only, this equity grows faster and eventually exponentially so.

Another way equity accrues to a home is through home price appreciation. As the home grows in value (thanks to natural area appreciation or home improvement projects) the equity in the property similarly grows. Equity is always a handy asset, which makes it an integral part of the person's aggregate net worth. In an emergency or on a rainy day, home owners can simply withdraw large lump sum amounts from the equity of the house one day. This wealth might also be simply passed along down the family line to the owners' heirs as well.

There are two principle ways to withdraw the equity value from a house. It might be taken as a home equity loan or a home equity line of credit (called a HELOC). Either one will allow an individual to utilize the proceeds for practically anything they wish. This might be for home improvements, vacations, retirement, or university level education as a few examples.

Income Statement

An Income Statement refers to a corporate financial statement that relays the performance of the company for a specific accounting time frame. Analysts measure such performance through reading the summary of the business revenues and expenditures in its non-operating and operating endeavors together. This statement reveals the net loss or net profit which the business experienced in the particular accounting time period. These documents are also referred to as statements of revenues or profit and loss statements.

As one of three important financial statements, these become contained within the yearly 10-K and corporate annual reports. The other two critical documents are the statement of cash flows and the balance sheet. Every publically traded firm is required by law to deliver such legal documents to the investing public via the SEC Securities and Exchange Commission. These three combined statements relay all of the critical information on the firm's financial affairs. Yet the income statement is special in that it alone reveals the company's net income and overall sales' overviews.

Income statements are different from the balance sheet in at least one critical way. Balance sheets provide a single moment in time snap shot of corporate performance. Income statements on the other hand deliver useful information on an entire time frame or period. They start with the company sales figures and conclude with the total net income and appropriate EPS earnings per share figures.

These income statements become sub-divided into two sections. The first is operating. The second proves to be non-operating. Operating sections of the statements on income reveal all of the pertinent data on expenses and revenues which result directly from the normal principal daily operations of the business. It helps to look at a real world example to better understand the concept. If a company makes computer equipment, then it will mostly earn its revenues through manufacturing and selling such computer equipment.

In the non-operating segment of the income statement, investors learn about the expenses and revenues associated with extraordinary operations of the firm. Continuing on with the prior example, the computer equipment firm may also sell some investments and real estate properties. Any and all gains it realizes on the sales would be included under the non-operating items portion of the statement.

Analysts find a number of important uses for these income statements. Among the key ones is figuring up critical financial ratios like ROA return on assets, ROE return on equity, gross and operating profits, EVIT earnings before interest and taxes, and EBITDA earnings before interest, taxes, and amortization. As such, these statements will commonly be portrayed in a standardized format that lays out every line item as a percentage of the sales. This method allows for analysts and investors alike to quickly and easily determine the expenses that comprise the greatest amount of the sales.

These statements may similarly compare and contrast both the QOQ quarter over quarter performance and the YOY year over year performance. This is why the income statement commonly delivers at least two and often three years of comparable historical data for analysts to consider. There are also two methods for presenting the income statements. They might be offered in a multi-step format. Accountants for the company could also portray them in a single step format. Each of the two methods is consistent with the important GAAP standards. They also both provide the identical net income final numbers. In fact their figures are formulated in more or less the same way. It is only their compilation and format which proves to be different from one another.

Inflation

Inflation proves to be prices rising over time. It is specifically measured as the increase in a given basket of goods and services' prices. These goods and services are taken to represent the entire economy. Inflation is also the going up in cost of the average prices of goods and services as measured by the CPI, or consumer price index. The opposite of inflation is known as deflation. Deflation turns out to be the falling of an average level of prices. The point that separates the two from each other, both deflation and inflation, is price stability, or no change in the costs of goods and services.

Inflation has almost everything to do with the amount of money available. It is inextricably tied to the money supply. This gives rise to the popularly remarked observation that inflation is actually an excessive number of dollars chasing too small a quantity of goods. Comprehending the way that this works is easier when considering an example.

Pretend for a moment that the world possessed only two commodities: oranges that are gathered up from orange trees and paper money created by government. In seasons where rain is limited and the oranges are few as a result, the cost of oranges should go up. This is because the same number of printed dollars would be competing for a smaller number of oranges.

On the other hand, if a bumper crop of oranges are seen, then the cost of oranges should drop, since the sellers of oranges have no choice but to cut prices to sell off their large inventory of oranges. These two examples illustrate inflation in the former and deflation in the latter. The main difference between the real world and this example is that inflation measures changes in the price movement on average of many or all goods and services, and not simply one.

The quantity of money in an economy similarly impacts the amount of inflation present at any given time. Should the government in the example above choose to print enormous amounts of money, then there will be many dollars for a relatively constant number of oranges, as in the lack of rain scenario. So inflation is created by the number of dollars going up against the quantities of oranges that exist, or overall goods and services existing. Deflation, as the opposite of inflation, would be the numbers of dollars dropping compared to the quantity of oranges available.

Because of this, levels of inflation result from four different factors that often work together in combination. The demand for money could drop. The supply of money could expand. The available supply of various other goods might decline. Finally, the demand for other goods increases.

Even though these four factors do work in correlation, economists say that inflation is mostly a currency driven event. This means that in the vast majority of cases, it results from governments tampering with the money supply. Generally, they do this by over printing their own currency to have money to pay for spending, resulting in higher inflation.

Initial Public Offering (IPO)

An IPO is the acronym for an Initial Public Offering. Such IPO's represent the first opportunity for most investors to start buying shares of stock in the firm in question. Initial Public Offerings commonly generate a great deal of excitement, not only for the company involved but also for the members of the investing community.

Private companies decide to issue stock and become publicly traded companies for a few different reasons. The main two motivating factors revolve around the need to raise more capital, as well as the desire to permit the original business owners and investors to take profits on their time and investment that they originally put into starting up the company.

It is true that private companies are limited in the amount of capital that they are able to raise, since their ownership turns out to be restricted to certain organizations and individuals. Public companies have the advantages of allowing any investor to take a stake through buying stock shares on exchanges that are publicly traded. It is far easier for them to raise money as public companies.

Initial Public Offerings that go well translate to large amounts of cash for a company. They use this for future expansion and development. Those who began the company or who were initial investors typically make enormous gains at that time in compensation for their time and effort.

Initial Public Offerings take huge amounts of preliminary work. Great amounts of paper work have to be filled in and filed with the regulatory oversight groups. A prospectus has to be created for investors to study and consider. Advertising campaigns for the first shares that will be sold must be developed. On top of these tasks, the company has to continue its normal operations. Because of this, financial firms such as Morgan Stanley or Goldman Sachs are commonly engaged to perform these tasks on the company's behalf. Such a firm is called the IPO underwriting company. With enormous sized IPO's, these tasks could even be divided up between a few different IPO underwriting companies.

Contrary to what many people think, the majority of IPO's typically do not do well initially. Besides this, a percentage of the companies will not make it, meaning that all of the investment in the IPO stock could be lost. Because of this, there is great risk and often lower rewards for sinking money into Initial Public Offerings than in traditional well established companies and stocks. Many investors buy into the enthusiasm and excitement that surrounds Initial Public Offerings. Another explanation for their euphoria may have to do with believing that there is something special in being among the first investors to acquire the next possible Apple, Coca Cola, or IBM. Whatever their reasoning proves to be, investors continue to love Initial Public Offerings and the somewhat long shot opportunities that they represent.

Insolvency

Insolvency refers to the point where an individual, business, or even governmental organization is not able to cover its various financial obligations any longer. This means that it is unable to settle debts with its creditors and lenders as they are due. Many times, before such an indebted individual, company, or government becomes embroiled in any type of insolvency or bankruptcy procedures, they will try to enter into informal negotiations with creditors. This could involve setting up other payment schedules and arrangements.

Insolvency can happen for a variety of reasons. Among these is a decrease in cash flow and profitability forecasts, poor management of cash resources, or a rapid expansion in costs and expenses. Where businesses are concerned, this type of insolvency is classified according to one of two separate categories. The first of these is Cash Flow insolvency. This happens as a corporation or company simply can not pay the business debts as they become due. The second form is Balance Sheet insolvency. This type results from a company reaching the point where it possesses a negative net asset position. It simply means that the corporation's aggregate debts are greater than its total assets.

It is entirely possible for firms to be solvent by balance sheet figures but at the same time be insolvent by cash flow. The opposite scenario could also occur. If a company is bankrupt according to its balance sheet while still solvent by cash flow, it simply means its incoming revenues permit it to cover its current financial obligations. There are numerous companies which possess longer term debt obligations that continuously operate in this balance sheet-bankrupt status.

Technically, insolvency and bankruptcy are not exactly the same thing. The former is a condition of being in financial trouble or at least difficulties. Bankruptcy is instead a court order. It describes the ways in which a debtor which is no longer solvent will continue to meet its obligations or instead have its assets sold off to settle with the creditors.

This means that it is entirely possible for a company, individual, or government entity to be no longer solvent but not yet be officially bankrupt.

This could result from a temporary or sometimes fixable problem. The reverse is never the case. An entity can not be bankrupt yet still be solvent. Such a lack of solvency often translates into an eventual bankrupt state when the debtors are not able to improve their financial conditions.

Corporations and firms that have become insolvent are able to improve their financial state. They might slash costs, borrow money, sell their assets, renegotiate the terms of their debts, or seek out a bigger corporation to acquire them. The buyer could settle their debts as part of the assumption of their services, products, technology, and proprietary trademarks.

Several unfortunate events can lead to a company becoming insolvent. If they do not have enough management in human resources or accounting departments, this could contribute to the problem. A lack of qualified accounting staff could cause a company's budget to be either ignored or misappropriated.

There might also be sharply increasing vendor prices which the company is powerless to stop. Higher prices for their goods and services mean that companies will have to raise their prices in an effort to pass these along to the consumer. The problem arises when customers then shop another company or product to get a better price. Lost clientele nearly always translates into a drop in cash flow. This means that they no longer have the cash coming in to cover the bills due to the company creditors.

There could also be lawsuits brought by employees or customers that break a company's finances. The firm could be forced to pay enormous bills for both defense and in settlement damages which make it impossible for them to continue ongoing operations. As operations cease and revenue naturally drops, the ability to pay bills disappears quickly.

A final reason centers on the lack of evolution in a company product line. It might be customers simply change their needs and therefore purchasing habits. This could lead them to rival firms which offer a broader product range or line. The company which could not or did not adapt its products will find its revenues and profits decreasing to the point where they are unable to cover their expenses with their remaining income.

Interest Rate

Interest rates are the levels at which interest is charged a borrower for using money that they obtain in the form of a loan from a bank or other lender. These are also the rates that individuals and businesses are paid for depositing their funds with a bank. Interest rates are central to the running of capitalist economies. They are commonly written out as percentage rates for a given time frame, most commonly per year.

As an example, a small business might require capital to purchase new assets for the company. To acquire these, they borrow money form a bank. In exchange for making them this loan, the bank is paid interest at a pre set and agreed upon rate of interest for lending it to the company and putting off their own use of the monies. They receive this interest in monthly payments along with repayments of the principal.

Interest rates are also used by government agencies in pursuing monetary policies. Central banks set them to influence their nation's economic performance. They impact many elements of an economy such as unemployment, inflation, and investment levels.

There are several different interest rates to consider. The most commonly expressed one is the nominal interest rate. This nominal interest rate proves to be the amount of interest that is payable in money terms. If a family deposits $1,000 in a bank for a year, and is paid $50 in interest, then their balance by the conclusion of the year will be $1,050. This would translate to a nominal interest rate amounting to five percent per year.

The real interest rate is another type of rate used to determine how much purchasing power is received. It is the interest rate after the level of inflation is subtracted. Determining the real interest rate is a matter of calculating the nominal rate and removing the amount of inflation from it. In the example above, supposed the economy's inflation level is measured at five percent for the year. This would mean that the $1,050 in the account at year end only buys what it did as $1,000 at the beginning of the year. This translates to a real interest rate of zero.

Interest rates change for many reasons. They are altered for political gains of parties in power. By reducing the interest rate, an economy gains a short term boost. The help to the economy will often influence the outcome of elections. Unfortunately, the short term advantage gained is often offset later by inflation. This reason for changing interest rates is eliminated with independent central banks.

Another main reason that interest rates change is because of expectations of inflation. Since the majority of economies demonstrate inflation, fixed amounts of money will purchase fewer goods a year from now than they will today. Lenders expect to be compensated for this. Central banks raise interest rates to fight this inflation as necessary.

Internal Revenue Service (IRS)

The Internal Revenue Service is an agency of the United States government. It is an entity that falls under the Department of the Treasury. The IRS' purpose is to collect incomes taxes from businesses and working individuals. Workers generally pay in their incomes taxes to the IRS once a year. There are cases where groups pay taxes quarterly, as with businesses and independent contractors who make more than pre-determined amounts. In practice employers withhold most individuals' taxes are from their paychecks.

For most individuals and small businesses, annual tax payments are due every year on April 15th. They pay these for the preceding year. Submitting these payments and forms is known as filing taxes with the IRS. The agency also permits extensions for filing if the requests are turned in ahead of the due date. Estimated payments have to come with the request for extension.

The Internal Revenue Service figures up taxes for individuals and businesses on a sliding scale. Individuals and entities that earn higher amounts are subsequently placed into higher tax brackets. The more individuals earn, the higher amount they will be required to pay to the IRS.

Any person who earns a yearly salary or who is paid wages by the hour will have taxes estimated and deducted directly from every payroll. This creates a situation where too much or too little money may be deducted throughout the year. Individuals who overpay will receive a refund. Those who underpay will have to make a payment to cover the additional tax if the appropriate amount did not come out of checks during the year.

Income taxes in the U.S. depend on the amount of net income. This is the income that remains once deductions have been calculated and subtracted from the total gross income. Individuals in the poverty bracket are not expected to pay any income taxes. Those people who earn $50,000 will pay around 20% of their net incomes. Over $100,000 earners are more likely to pay near 25% of net income earned. Sometimes those earning millions of dollars per year are able to use tax shelters, business write offs, and accounting strategies to receive substantial tax breaks and actually pay a lower percentage of their net income in taxes. This is why the middle class in America bears the greatest taxation burden.

The IRS was not the original Federal taxing authority in the United States. President Lincoln began its original predecessor the Bureau of Internal Revenue in 1862 with Congressional approval. They set this agency up to collect a new income tax to assist in paying for the Civil War. This tax was intended and enacted to be temporary at the time.

While the first income tax did become repealed in 1872, the government reinstated it again in 1894. Supreme Court legal challenges kept the income tax in a quasi legal state until the 16th Amendment came into force in 1913 and allowed income taxes to be permanent. Eventually the Bureau of Internal Revenue evolved into the Internal Revenue Service.

The IRS website offers consumers and businesses all of their forms in a convenient, downloadable format. It also features instructional pages to properly complete these tax forms. A frequently asked questions page helps individuals with general queries. For people who need assistance in filing, there are a variety of software programs available that will ask questions and prepare the relevant tax forms for individuals. These programs then file the forms online with the IRS. Another option is to hire and pay a CPA certified public accountant to complete and file their tax forms.

Investor

Strictly speaking, an investor is any person or entity that makes an investment. In the past, the word investors has acquired a far more specific meaning. In the world of business and finance, investors has come to characterize those individuals or companies that routinely buy debt instruments like bonds, or equity issues like stocks in an attempt to make financial profits. They hope to realize such gains in return for financing or providing capital to a company that is looking to expand.

Investors also relates to other types of individuals, businesses, or parties that put money into different types of investments. Although this is a less commonly used version of the word investors, it can relate to those engaging in currency, real estate, commodities, derivatives, or other personal property investments like art or antiques. An example of this would be a real estate investor. They purchase a piece of property or a house with the hopes of selling it for a greater amount of money than for what they purchased it. Similarly, commodities' investors are hoping to buy contracts or options on hard assets like gold, oil, or lumber cheaply to sell them later more dearly.

Investors are commonly buying such stocks, bonds, or other types of assets and holding on to them with the goal of realizing one of two types of returns, or in some unusual cases both types. These are capital gains or cash flow investments. Investors who are interested in capital gains are simply looking to sell an instrument or asset that they obtained at one price for a greater amount. When they do this, they realize a capital gain. Should they sell the investment for less than they purchased it, they would instead realize a capital loss. Capital gains can only be realized one time on an investment, as the investors will have sold the investment and have to look for another investment to begin the process anew once again.

Cash flow investors are alternatively looking for a repetitive income stream. They hope to achieve regular, smaller sums of passive income just from holding their investment. Dividends on a stock, royalties on an oil or gas investment, and rents from a residential or commercial realty property are all examples of cash flow investments and returns. So long as the investor owns the cash flow investment, he or she should be able to continuously count on a regular income stream.

The word investor commonly gives the connotation of a person who acquires these assets for the longer term. This stands in contrast to a day trader or even short term investor. Investors can be professional or self taught amateurs.

Investors also represent many entities other than individuals or even traditional businesses. They can be investment groups like clubs, venture capital investors who provide money to start up companies, investment banks, investment trusts such as REIT Real Estate Investment Trusts, hedge funds and mutual funds, and even sovereign wealth funds that invest on behalf of their respective nations.

Lease

Leases are contracts made between an owner, or lessor, and a user, or lesee, covering the utilization of an asset. Leases can pertain to business or real estate. There are a variety of different types of leases that vary with the property in question being leased.

Tangible property and assets are leased under rental agreements. Intangible property leases are much like a license, only they have differing provisions. The utilization of a computer program or a cell phone service's radio frequency are two example of such an intangible lease.

A gross lease is another type of lease. In a gross lease, a tenant actually gives a certain defined dollar amount in rent. The landlord is then responsible for any and all property expenses that are routinely necessary in owning the asset. This includes everything from washing machines to lawnmowers.

You also encounter leases that are cancelable. Cancelable leases can be ended at the discretion of the end user or lessor. Other leases are non cancelable and may not be ended ahead of schedule. In daily conversation, a lease denotes a lease that can not be broken, while a rental agreement often can be canceled.

A lease contract typically lays out particular provisions concerning both rights and obligations of the lessor and the lessee. Otherwise, a local law code's provisions will apply. When the holder of the lease, also known as the tenant, pays the arranged fee to the owner of the property, the tenant gains exclusive use and possession of the property that is leased to the point that the owner and any other individuals may not utilize it without the tenant's specific invitation. By far the most typical type of hard property lease proves to be the residential types of rental agreements made between landlords and their tenants. This type of relationship that the two parties establish is also known as a tenancy. The tenant's right to possess the property is many times referred to as the leasehold interest. These leases may exist for pre arranged amounts of time, known as a lease term. In many cases though, they can be terminated in advance, although this does depend on the particular lease's terms and conditions.

Licenses are similar to leases, but not the same thing. The main difference between the two lies in the nature of the ongoing payments and termination. When keeping the property is only accomplished by making regular payments, and can not be terminated unless the money is not paid or some form of misconduct is discovered, then the agreement is a lease. One time uses of or entrances to property are licenses. The defining difference between the two proves to be that leases require routine payments in their term and come with a particular date of ending.

Ledger

A Ledger is also often called a general ledger. It refers to a firm's set of (numbered) accounts that it maintains for its corporate accounting records. With such a record, the firm has a full history of all its financial transactions it has entered into throughout the entire existence of the firm. In this master set of company books, the firm keeps all of the necessary information it must have to compile its financial statements. The data will always cover such useful facts and figures as liabilities, assets, cash flow and positions, revenues, expenses, profits, and owners' equity.

Accountants work with these general ledgers as part of their book keeping system for drawing up the company financial statements. All transactions must be included in the master document. Accountants will first pursue creating a trial balance. This represents a report of all account balances and the corresponding accounts. It is this adjusted trial balance which will be employed to create all relevant corporate financial statements.

These general ledgers are employed continuously by those firms which utilize the method of book keeping known as the double entry system. In such a methodology of accounting, every financial transaction will impact minimally two different ledgers and accounts. It also signifies that every entry will have an equal and opposite credit and debit transaction. Such double entries will be arrayed in two separate columns. Generally the debit postings will be to the left while the credit entries will be posted to the right column. It is imperative that all credit and debit entries balance out all the time.

It helps to look at a concrete example to better understand this challenging concept. When a customer pays a $300 invoice, the cash account will rise. The accountant will book a $300 credit to cash. At the same time, he or she will then log a $300 debit on the other column for the accounts receivable. In this way, both the credits and debits will equal out.

There are four key financial statements which accountants can produce from these general ledgers. The balance sheet is one of them. Under balance sheets there are sub divisions including accounts receivable and cash accounts reports. The formula for any balance sheet proves to be assets minus liabilities equals equity. The one cash account in the example above gains by $300 while the accounts receivable category becomes reduced by the amount of $300. Thanks to this simultaneous increasing and decreasing of the balance sheet equation left side, the equation will stay in perfect balance.

A second critical financial report which is impacted by the general ledgers proves to be the income statement. It also has a formula, which amounts to revenue minus expenses equals net income (also called profit). It is crucial that this formula similarly remains balanced for the financial statements to be correct. A single given transaction might also affect both the income statement and the balance sheet. Consider another example. Firms might bill their clients $750. They would note a $750 debit on to the accounts receivable category. At the same time, they would put up a $750 credit on to the revenue (or cash) categories. Both the credits and debits grow by $750 this way. The two totals remain in balance.

This double entry accounting contrasts with single entry accounting methods. In either methodology of book keeping, the common element will be the accountant or book keeper working with a general ledger of some type.

Lender

Lenders are individuals or more commonly institutions that loan out money. The person who receives this money is a borrower. A number of different kinds of lending organizations exist. These include commercial, mutual organizations, educational, hard money, and lenders of last resort.

Commercial lenders are the most common of the traditional lenders. Commercial types are usually banks. Another kind of commercial lender would be a private financial organization. Commercial lenders provide offers on their loans to their borrowers at a set rate of loan terms. Such terms include time frame of the loan and the interest rate. Their goal is to make as much money as possible relative to the chances of the borrower not repaying the loan.

Mutual organizations are another type of lender. They are composed of members of the mutual who cooperate together to loan money to the membership. The members pool their money into the organization. From there it is loaned out to the members who need to borrow money. They do this with favorable terms and at advantageous rates.

Mutual organizations are not driven to make profits. This allows them to offer lower interest rates on the loans they make and higher interest rates on the deposits they take. Among these mutual groups are community based credit unions. Friendly Societies are another example of them.

Educational lenders provide loans to individuals who are looking to further their education at an institution of higher learning like a college or university. They offer borrowers subsidized or unsubsidized loans. When the loans are subsidized, the Federal Government guarantees the loans and ensures that the lender provides a low and often fixed interest rate.

Hard money lenders make special types of loans that are short term. These are loans principally secured by real estate collateral. The downside to this kind of a lender is that they often provide higher interest rates than a traditional commercial bank. The tradeoff is that they will often take on a larger variety of deals.

Typically these hard money lenders give terms that are more flexible to their borrowers. Some states have stricter laws on interest rates that may be charged than does the Federal government. This forces hard money lenders to operate under different rules and with lower interest rates when they are in conflict with usury laws in give states.

Many times these loans that lenders make to individuals become brokered loans. In such cases, third parties consider the borrower's case then send the loan request out to a variety of lenders. This is often done over the Internet. They pick these different lenders because of their chance of approving the borrower in question. Sometimes the terms can be improved by one or more of these competing lenders in order to win over the borrower's business.

Lenders of last resort are an interesting final category. They are often governmental organizations whose goal is to save national economies and important banks from failure. These types of organizations loan money out to too big to fail banks which are close to collapse. They do this to safeguard the bank's depositors and to prevent panic from pushing the nation's economy into a downward spiral.

Lenders of last resort can also be private organizations that make loans to individuals. These groups loan out money to borrowers who present great risks of default or who have extremely low credit scores. Interest rates with these lenders are substantially higher than with traditional lenders. They charge these rates in order to make up for the losses they suffer from their borrower's greater default rates. Such lenders that charge even higher rates are sometimes known as loan sharks.

Liabilities

Where a business is concerned, liabilities prove to be amounts of money that are owed by the company at any given point. These liabilities are displayed on the firm's balance sheet. They are commonly listed as items payable, or simply as payables.

There are two types of liabilities. These are longer term liabilities and shorter term liabilities. Long term liabilities turn out to be business obligations that last for greater than the period of a single year. Mortgages payable and loans payable are included in this category.

Short term liabilities represent business obligations that will be paid in less than a year. There are many different kinds of short term liabilities. They include all of the items detailed below.

Payroll taxes payable are one of these. They represent sums automatically collected from the employees and put to the side by the employer. They have to be given to the IRS and any state taxing agencies at the pre determined time.

Sales taxes payable are another short term liability. The business collects them from its customers when sales are made. They hold them until it is time to give them to the proper revenue collecting department within the state.

Mortgages and loans payable are another short term liability. These represent payments made every month on mortgages and loans. They are not large single payments or the total amount of a loan that is eventually owed, but instead represent recurring monthly obligations.

Liabilities for individuals are another type of liabilities altogether. They also represent money that has to be paid out. For people, they are debts owed, as well as monthly cash flow that goes out of the individual's accounts.

Liabilities and assets are the opposites of each other, yet people often get them confused. While assets are things that contribute positive cash flow to a person's finances, liabilities are those that create negative cash flow, or money that leaves an individual's accounts every month. For example, a house that an individual owes money on and makes monthly payments on is a liability, not an asset. The house takes money from the person in the form of monthly mortgage payments each month. For a house to be an asset, it would have to be completely paid off. Even still, if monthly taxes and insurance payments are being made, then technically it would still be a liability. Houses can only be assets really and truly when they are rented out and the rental income that a person receives is greater than all of the expenses associated with the house every month, including any mortgage payments, taxes, insurance, upkeep, and property management fees. When the net result of a property is money coming in, then it is an asset and not a liability.

Lien

A lien is a claim on one individual's property by another person or entity. The party that holds the lien is able to recover the property if a debtor will not follow through with making payments. There are also other circumstances in which liens would allow the lien holder to take the property. Mortgages on houses or buildings prove to be one kind these. Vehicle loans for a business or individual represent other types that are put on the value of the vehicle. When the obligation is paid off, the lien becomes discharged.

Before individuals are able to receive their money after the sale of an asset like a car or house, the lien must be paid off first. With a vehicle, this means that the lender will not send out the title until they receive complete repayment of the principal.

The majority of liens allow for the individuals or businesses to utilize the property as they are paying it. There are scenarios where the lender or creditor physically holds the property while the borrower is making payments. These are a part of bankruptcy procedures as well because they are secured loans with debt repayment rules that have to be addressed in a case.

While there are a number of different types of liens, the most typical one is on a vehicle. Individuals buy a car from the dealer. The bank loans the money and secures the loan. They do this by placing a vehicle lien which allows them to hold on to the automobile's title. The lender files a UCC-1 form to record this. So long as the debtor continues to make payments, the loan will be paid off finally. The bank would then release to the individual the title.

If the individuals stop making their payments, the bank is able to take possession of the vehicle back while still holding the title. If the vehicle owners choose to sell the automobile when they still owe principal, they must clear the bank loan in order to obtain the title. Without the title, a person can not sell the vehicle.

There are a variety of different types of liens in the world. Consensual ones are those which individuals voluntarily accept when they buy something. Non consensual ones are also known as statutory. These come from a court process where an entity places a lien on assets because bills have not been paid. Three of these are fairly common.

A tax lien occurs when individuals do not pay local, state, or federal income taxes. These are put on the offender's property. A judgment lien comes as a result of a case in a small claims court. When a court gives a judgment to one party, the offending party might refuse to pay. In this case the court will place a judgment lien on the offender's property.

A mechanic or contractor lien happens when a contractor performs a job for a home owner. If the owner refuses to pay, the contractor can ask a court to place a lien on the property in question. This would have to be paid off along with other security interests before the property owner is able to sell.

Liquidity

Liquidity refers to the point that a security or asset is able to be sold or bought in a given marketplace without interfering with the price of the asset. Good liquidity is demonstrated through a great amount of trading activity. Liquid assets prove to be the kinds that are simply and quickly able to be purchased and sold. Liquidity can be summed up in a single sentence as the capability of rapidly turning an asset into cash.

Although no single means of determining liquidity exists, liquidity can be figured up through utilizing liquidity ratios. It is generally accepted that investing money in liquid assets proves to be safer and more accessible than placing your money into illiquid ones. The reason for this is that you are able to withdraw your money from a liquid investment quickly and without obstacles.

There are many types of assets that prove to be simply convertible into cash. Money Market accounts are some of the most liquid assets. Blue chip stocks turn out to be the most liquid of stocks traded.

Liquidity also has other meanings for businesses and economics. A business' capability of fulfilling its payment responsibilities is referred to as its liquidity. This is figured both with regards to the company having enough liquid assets that they are able to get to in a timely fashion.

The most liquid asset is money in your hand. This can be utilized right away for all economic functions. Among these are selling, buying, taking care of immediate needs and desires, and paying down debts.

In general, liquid assets possess many or at least a few of a number of features in common. These assets that have good liquidity are able to be sold at any point during market operating hours, quickly, and with as small a loss in value as possible. Markets with liquidity possess numerous sellers and buying who are both willing and able to transact at all times that the market is open. For markets to have deep liquidity, eager and willing parties in great numbers have to be present in a market all of the time that it is open.

The liquidity of a market has much to do with its market depth. Market depth is able to be quantified as the number of individual units that may be purchased or sold for a certain price impact. The opposite of this related term market depth is market breadth. Market breadth is quantified as the amount of price impact for every unit of such liquidity.

A given item's liquidity is measurable in terms of how frequently it is sold or purchased. This is called volume. Investments in markets with great volume like futures markets and the stock markets are generally understood to have far greater liquidity than do real estate markets. This is simply a function of stocks and futures' capability of being rapidly transacted.

There are assets that possess even liquid secondary markets. These offer greater advantages for traders, and because of this, buyers will pay a greater price for such an asset than for an asset that is similar but does not possess a liquid secondary market. This liquidity discount proves to be the lowered anticipated return or guaranteed yield on these kinds of assets.

An example of this is the variance between just issued U.S. Treasury bonds and treasuries that are no longer recently issued. Both may have the same amount of time until they mature, but investors are more interested in purchased the ones that have only just been issued. Because of this, these newest ones have a higher price and lower yield.

Mortgage

Mortgages are loans made on commercial or residential properties. They commonly use the house or the property itself as collateral. These mortgages are paid off in monthly installments over the course of a pre determined amount of time. Mortgages commonly come in fifteen, twenty, and thirty year periods, though both longer ones and shorter ones are available.

A variety of differing mortgages exist. All of them have their own terms and conditions that translate into advantages and disadvantages. Among the various mortgage types are fixed rate mortgages, adjustable rate mortgages, and balloon payment mortgages.

The most common kinds or mortgages, especially for first time home buyers, prove to be fixed rate mortgages. This is the case because they are both simple to understand and extremely stable. With such a mortgage, the regular monthly payments will be the same during the entire life of the loan. This makes them very predictable and manageable. Fixed rate mortgages have the advantages of protection against inflation, since the interest rate is locked in and can not go up with the floating interest rates. They allow for longer term planning. They come with very low risk, since you are always aware of both the payment and interest rate.

Adjustable rate mortgages, also known as ARM's, have become more popular since they begin with lower, more manageable interest rates that result in a lower initial monthly payment. The downside to them is that the interest rate can and likely will go up and down in the loan's life time. Factors to consider with ARM's are the adjustment periods, the indexes and margins, and the caps ceilings, and floors. The adjustment period is the one in which the interest rate is allowed to reset, commonly starting anywhere from six months to ten years after the mortgage begins.

The interest rates change based on the index and margin. The interest rates are actually based on an index that is published, whether it is the London Interbank Offered Rate, or LIBOR, or the U.S. Constant Maturity Treasury, or CMT. The margin is added to this index to determine the total new interest rate on your mortgage. The amount that these ARM rates are capable of going up or down in a single adjustment period and for the life of the loan is called a cap, a ceiling or a floor.

The third common type of mortgages is balloon reset mortgages. They come with thirty year schedules for repayment, with a caveat. Unless you pay are willing to allow the mortgage to reset to then current interest rates at the end of either a five year or seven year term, then your entire balance will be due at this point. This gives you the benefits of the low monthly payment plan as a person with a thirty year loan would have, yet you will have to be willing to pay off the whole mortgage if you do not take the reset option when the term is up. Because of this, many people refer to this type of a mortgage as a two step mortgage.

Net Worth

Net worth is a figure that represents a business, an individual, or another group's difference between the assets that they have and the liabilities that they owe. Figuring up this net worth is done by first taking all of the entity's debts and obligations and then subtracting that number from the entire sum of assets. If the total of all of these assets is greater than the sum of all of the debts and obligations, then a positive net worth results. Otherwise, when the debts are greater than the assets, then the entity has a negative net worth.

When you sit down to determine the net worth figure, every asset should be totaled in the operation. There are many different kinds of assets. These are comprised of cash in the bank, holdings of stocks, real estate, bonds, and other types of investments, and major possessions like vehicles. Correctly figuring out the different assets' values is done with the use of the up to date fair market value, not the cost paid for the item when it is purchased.

You must also correctly add up the total of debts and obligations when you are attempting to get a correct net worth value. Liabilities cover many different obligations, like a car payment, mortgage, total of credit card debt outstanding, and any other forms of loans that have balances left on them. Both every asset and liability must be measured in order to come up with an accurate net worth.

Knowing your present net worth is very useful and meaningful. If you are able to cover all of your outstanding debt obligations simply by selling of all of your assets, then you have a financial condition that is fairly stable and in order. If your assets are more than sufficient to cover all of your obligations, then your finances are in greater shape. Most businesses and people seek to reach a point that they have actual positive net worth.

There are a few benefits from having a correct understanding of your net worth. It is essential that your present assets' value is greater than your present debt load. A person who owes more money than they actually own presents a profile of a person who is not an especially good credit risk. Without a positive net worth, many lending institutions like banks will think twice about providing you with the most advantageous loan rates offered. This is because they feel that you present more of a risk to lend money.

It is also good to know where your net worth stands because it is a helpful beginning point for your general financial planning. Should you discover that you hardly have sufficient assets with which to cover your present amount of debts, then this is a good sign that you should not engage in any other purchases until later, after you have eliminated several of your debts. This means that if you occasionally figure up your net worth, then you will comprehend not only where you stand now, but also when you will be in a better position to purchase a new car.

Operating Expenses

In the world of business and corporations, operating expenses is the term that pertains to the continuous costs of running a business. This makes operating expenses the expenses for everything happening behind the scenes. Such operating costs include any expenses incurred for the literal operation of the business.

You occasionally see the words operating expenses written as OPEX. This is especially true in internal memos and documentation that are relevant to the earnings of a company. The most frequent operating expenses are those having to do with employee benefits and salaries. These commonly make up the biggest individual expenses for a corporation. Other operating costs could be office supplies, marketing budgets, licensing and legal fees, raw material expenses, costs of research and development, accounting fees, and office utilities.

Another key operating expense is depreciation. Depreciation proves to be the quantity of value that diminishes in an asset over a period of time. This means that accounts can take equipment, vehicles, and other assets and subtract out the lower value off of the initial value to come up with depreciation as assets gradually lose value. This depreciation can be counted as an operating expense so long as the asset is still employed by the business in its operations.

Some expenses are deemed to be capital expenses instead of operating expenses. This is generally the case for single event expenses, like buying replacement equipment for completely depreciated existing equipment. This division of costs allows both the firm and its investors to have a more realistic snap shot of for what the money is used before it is able to be put to profits. When you are self employed, then you may count both CAPEX and OPEX as business expenses.

Operating expenses have to be included in the annual reports of both not for profit outfits and corporations that are publicly traded. This kind of information commonly comes with charts that compare the operating expenses of several years. In this way, a reader is able to obtain a good understanding of how the expenses are progressing with time.

By tracking operating expenses in an ongoing fashion all year long, the information is easily at hand for a company to include it in their reports. Accountants, or alternatively programs that do financial management, are generally used to help with operating expense tracking and calculation. When operating expenses go up and down every year, investors will want to know why this is the case. Detailed records provide good explanations for the final numbers to satisfy the questioning parties. Corporate treasurers are generally responsible for answering these queries and coming up with answers.

Passive Income

Passive income refers to money that, once it is arranged and established, does not require additional work from the person getting it. A variety of different types of passive income exist. Among them are movie, music, book, screenplay, television, and patent royalties. Other samples of passive income include click through income, rental income, and revenue from online advertising.

Activities that lead to passive income have something in common. They usually need a great amount of money, time, or both invested in them upfront to get them started. There are financial means to establishing passive income as well. You could purchase a rental property or choose to invest in a partnership or other form of company where you are a silent partner. The income that you derive from these investment activities is deemed to be passive.

Various other kinds of passive income do not need a great deal of financial investment made in them, but instead require great amounts of effort, time, and even creativity to achieve. More than a year can be required to either build up a popular website that can contribute passive income from advertising or to write a great novel. Making money from such passive income that is actually profit may take longer.

Books are a good example of how long it can take to actually make money from passive income. Publishers generally get to recover all of their printing and promoting costs, as well as any advance monies given to authors, before royalties are created and paid. Books that sell poorly could turn out to pay the author little to nothing.

Websites have a different set of challenges for their creators. There has to be more than simply good content to make money from them. They must similarly rank high in the search engine results for the necessary amount of visitors to find and go to the website. Unless a great number of visitor hits are recorded on a website, the passive income that is generated will be negligible or even none.

People are willing to put in such a huge amount of time with little assurance of results because they know that the passive income generating activity will create money for them around the clock for years to come, if it is successful. This means that passive income money is constantly being made, even when the person is asleep or on vacation. If you are able to get one passive income project up and running well, then you can attempt others. This way, you might hope to develop a few different income streams that result in a significant annual revenue which can even support you.

Many investors believe that passive income is the most superior kind that you can achieve. This is why rental properties can be so popular. Even though they can require a significant amount of maintenance work and tenant management, they can provide substantial income once several such properties are owned and made profitable.

Portfolio

In the world of business and finance, a portfolio stands for an investment collection that a person or institution holds. People and other entities put together portfolios in order to diversify their holdings to reduce risk to a manageable level. A number of different kinds of risk are mitigated through the acquisition of a few varying types of assets. A portfolio's assets might be comprised of stocks, options, bonds, bank accounts, gold certificates, warrants, futures contracts, real estate, facilities of production, and other assets that tend to hold their value.

Investment portfolios may be constructed in various ways. Financial entities will commonly do their own careful analysis of investments in putting together a portfolio. Individuals might work with the either financial firms or financial advisors that manage portfolios. Alternatively, they could put together a self directed portfolio through working with a self directed online broker such as TD Ameritrade, eTrade, or Scott Trade.

A whole field of portfolio management has arisen to help with the allocation of investment money. This management pertains to determining the types of assets that are appropriate for an individual's risk tolerance and ultimate goals. Choosing the instruments that will comprise a portfolio has much to do with knowing the kinds of instruments to buy and sell, how many of each to obtain, and the time that is most appropriate to purchase or sell them.

Such decisions are rooted in a measurement for the investments' performance. This usually pertains to risk versus return on investments and anticipated returns of the entire portfolio. With portfolio returns, various types of assets are understood to commonly return amounts of differing ranges. Portfolio management has to factor in an individual investor's own precise situation and desired results as well. There are investors who are more fearful of risk than are other investors. These kinds of investors are termed risk averse. Risk averse portfolios are significantly different in their composition than are typical portfolios.

Mutual funds have evolved the act of portfolio management almost to a science. Their fund managers came up with techniques that allow them to prioritize and ideally set their portfolio holdings. This fund management reduces risk and increases returns to maximum levels. Strategies that these managers have created for running portfolios include designing equally weighted portfolios, price weighted portfolios, capitalization weighted portfolios, and optimal portfolios in which the risk adjusted return proves to be the highest possible.

Well diversified portfolios will contain many different asset classes. These will include far more than just stocks, bonds, and mutual funds. They will feature international stocks and bonds to provide diversification away from the U.S. dollar, as well as foreign currencies and hard asset commodities such as real estate investments, and gold and silver holdings.

Portfolio Income

Portfolio income proves to be money that is actually brought in from a group of investments. The portfolio commonly includes all of the various types of investments that an investor owns. These include bonds, stocks, mutual funds, and certificates of deposit. These various financial instruments earn a variety of different types of passive income, such as dividends, interest income, and capital gain distributions. Such portfolio income returns are generated by the holdings of the various investment products in the portfolio.

Portfolio income varies with the types of investments that an investor picks. You as an investor will commonly look at two different factors when assembling a portfolio for portfolio income. These turn out to be the money that the investment itself will produce, which is also known as an investment's return, and the investment's risk level that it contains.

As an example, stocks are frequently deemed to be investments with considerable risk, yet the other side of the risk return equation is that they provide income from a company's dividends, or distribution earnings returned to the shareholders, as well as an increase in the stock price as the stock value gains with time. Certificates of deposit and bonds create interest income that is paid out on the investment that you hold. Still different kinds of investments produce other types of income, although this depends on the characteristics of the investment in question.

To maximize the portfolio income while reducing the amount of risk involved, individuals commonly choose to invest in numerous different kinds of investments. This is known as diversifying your portfolio and portfolio income. This way, you can combine both safer investments that provide lower real returns with riskier investments that offer greater investment returns. Your total collection of investments is the portfolio that makes your portfolio income for you.

This portfolio income is also classified as passive income, or income that does not require you to perform any work in order to make the money. The upfront investment actually creates the income without you having to be actively involved in the money making process. This stands in contrast to incomes that are earned through active involvement, or active income that you must expend both energy and time to create.

The ultimate goal for you with your portfolio income will probably be to build up enough of it that you are capable of living off of only the income that the portfolio generates. Once this point is reached, you would be able to not receive a payroll check any longer. Instead, you would support yourself in retirement from the dividends, interest, and capital gains created by the investments in the form of portfolio income. The best and safest way to do this is to only draw on the portfolio income itself, without drawing down the original principal.

By not touching the investment principal, you allow your portfolio and resulting portfolio income to build up over time. If you do not take out the portfolio income, then the total value of the portfolio will grow faster with time, allowing you to compound your investments for retirement. It is critical to have enough money saved for retirement that you do not need to take out this principal to support yourself. Sufficient portfolio income should be generated to cover the monthly retirement expenses. In this way, you will not be reducing your principal and risking the very real danger of your portfolio running out of money while you are still alive to need it.

Power of Attorney

A power of attorney is an agreement in writing that grants another individual the authority to make some choices if the grantor is not available. This person who receives the power does not have to be an attorney. Attorneys are typically only involved in drafting up or potentially witnessing such an agreement. The phrase comes from an individual receiving status as an agent or attorney in fact.

When people implement such a power of attorney they do not lose the ability to make their own decisions. Instead they are allowing another individual to act for them in matters specified within the written text. This can be very helpful if people are out of the country or in the hospital as an example. Someone else with this authority would be able to cash checks at the bank or pay bills on their behalf. It is simply a matter of sharing power with another person. The agent is only carrying out the grantor's wishes, not actually making choices for them, so long as they are coherent and mentally capable.

People who will be out of town for an extended period of time might find these arrangements particularly useful. With a power of attorney, the agent could carry out major decisions such as selling cars or other personal assets. The Internet has eliminated the need for some of these functions as computers and mobile devices make it possible for people to buy and sell stocks and handle many financial transactions from anywhere they have an online connection. There are still cases where a transaction will require an in person agent to handle them.

There is also a special kind of power of attorney that is used by individuals who lose their ability to handle decisions for their personal financial affairs. This is known as a durable power of attorney. In this case, the word durable refers to the ability of the agent to make the choices on the grantor's behalf when he or she can not mentally do them. This type of arrangement grants the agent the legal authority and responsibility to make the best possible physical and financial decisions for the grantor.

It means that the agent is able to spend the individual's money as appropriate, cash checks, deposit checks, and even withdraw money from the personal bank accounts. The agent further gains the authority to sign contracts, sell personal property, take legal actions, and file and follow up on insurance claims.

When people decide to enter a durable power of attorney arrangement, a notary public or lawyer should witness the document before they sign and execute it. If such individuals need to have a durable agreement established and are not mentally able to do it, courts can do this for them as they deem necessary.

Agents who become appointed to this position are expected to keep correct and segregated records on each transaction they perform. The records must also be easily available at all times. When the individual dies, his or her power of attorney becomes null and void. The will is responsible for the dispensation of the deceased person's estate.

Powers of attorney can be rescinded. If individuals feel unhappy in the ways that their agent is managing their personal affairs, they can simply revoke the authority back at any point. It is always wise for people to choose an individual to be agent whom they know and implicitly trust.

Prime Rate

The Prime Rate is the most typically utilized shorter term interest rate for the United State banking system. All kinds of lending institutions in the United States employ this U.S. benchmark interest rate as a basis or index rate to price their medium term to short term loans and products. This includes credit unions, thrifts, savings and loans, and commercial banks.

This makes the Prime Rate consistent around the country as banks strive to be competitive and profitable in their lending rates which they provide to both consumers and businesses. A universal rate like this simplifies the task for businesses and consumers as they shop around comparable loan products that competing banks offer. Every state in the country does not maintain its own benchmark rate. This makes a California Prime or New York Prime identical to the U.S. Prime.

Commercial and other banks charge this benchmark rate to their best customers. These are those clients who have the best credit ratings and loan history with the bank. Most of the time banks' best clients are made up of large companies.

The prime interest rate is also known as the prime lending rate. Banks typically base it on the Federal Reserve's federal funds rate. This is actually the rate that banks loan money to each other for overnight purposes. Retail customers also need to be aware of the prime lending rate. It directly impacts the lending rates that they can access for personal and small business loans as well as for home mortgages.

The federal government and Federal Reserve Bank do not set the prime lending rates. The individual banks set it. They then utilize this base rate or reference rate to set the prices for a great number of loans such as credit card loans and small business loans.

The Federal Reserve Board releases a statistics called "Selected Interest Rates." This is their survey of the prime interest rate as the majority of the twenty-five biggest banks set it. It is this publication which reveals the Prime Rate periodically. This is why the Federal Reserve does not directly set this important benchmark rate. The banks more or less base it on the target level of the federal funds rate that the Federal Open Market Committee sets and changes at their monthly meetings.

Different banks adjust their prime lending rate at the same time. The point where they change it is generally when the Federal Open Market Committee adjusts their own important Fed Funds Rate. Many publications refer to this periodically changing reference rate as the Wall Street Prime Rate.

A great number of consumer loans as well as commercial loans and credit card rates find their basis in the prime lending rate. Among these are car loans, home equity loans, personal and home lines of credit, and various kinds of personal loans.

The rates above the prime lending rate that banks charge their less then prime (or subprime) customers depend on the credit worthiness of the borrower in question. The banks attempt to correctly ascertain the risk of default for the borrower. For the best credit customers who have lower chances of defaulting, banks can afford to assess them a lower interest rate than others. Customers with higher chances of defaulting on their loans pay larger interest rates because of the risk associated with their loans not being repaid.

As of June 15, 2016, the Federal Open Market Committee voted to maintain its target fed funds rate in a range of from .25% to .5%. As a result of this, the U.S. prime lending rate stayed at 3.5%. Once per month the Federal Reserve committee meets to determine if they will change the fed funds rate.

Principal

Principal has several different meanings. It most commonly pertains to the initial amount of money that a person either invests or borrows with a loan. A secondary meaning has to do with a bond and its face value. Sometimes the word pertains to the owners of a company or the main participants in any type of transaction.

Where borrowing is concerned, this term relates to the upfront amount of any loan. It also is utilized to describe original amounts which the individuals still owe on the loan in question. Looking at a clear example always helps to clarify the concept. When people obtain a $100,000 mortgage, this Principal is the same $100,000. As the individuals pay down $60,000 of this amount, the remainder of $40,000 that is left to pay off is similarly referred to as Principal.

It is the original Principal that decides how much interest borrowers will pay. If borrowers take out a loan with an initial amount equaling $20,000 that comes with a yearly interest rate at seven percent, then they would be required to pay $1,400 in annual interest for each year that the loan remains open. As borrowers pay the monthly payments to the loan servicer, the interest charges for the month will first be paid off. What remains goes toward the initial amount which the individuals borrowed. Paying down this original amount borrowed remains the only means of lowering the interest amount that accrues on a monthly basis.

Another form of mortgage that operates differently has the name of zero principal mortgages. Bankers think of these as interest-only loans. They represent a unique form of financing where the routine monthly payments of the borrower only apply to the loan's interest. This means that the initial loan amount never gets paid down unless the borrower makes extra payments. It also translates to no equity building up in the property which backs the mortgage loan.

Because of this, financial advisors will typically not recommend these types of mortgages to home buyers as they are rarely in the true interest of the purchaser. Despite this fairly obvious assessment, there are a few unusual cases when they could work out for certain people. When a home buyer is starting out on a career path that pays very little initially but will later on earn substantially more in the not too distant future, it could be worthwhile to lock in the home price now while it is lower. Once the income increases apace, the borrowers always have the ability to refinance into a more traditional mortgage which would cover payments on the initial amounts borrowed as well.

Another scenario where these loans make sense relates to unusual and fantastic opportunities for a particular real estate investment deal. When huge returns on investment dollars can be anticipated, it is practical to go with these mortgage's far lower payments that are interest-only. Meanwhile the borrower can plow the additional monthly payment money savings into the exceptional investment opportunity.

Principal also finds use describing the first initial outlay on an investment. This does not take into consideration any interest that builds up or earnings on the investment. Savers might deposit $20,000 at a bank in a savings account with interest. After a number of years, the balance will grow to $21,500. The principal remains the original $20,000 the savers gave the bank. The additional $1,500 will be called interest or earnings on top of this initial outlay.

It is interesting to note that inflation will not change the nominal value of a loan or financial instrument's principal. Yet the effects of inflation do very much reduce the real value of the initial amount.

Promissory Note

Promissory notes are negotiable instruments that are called notes payable in accounting circles. In such promissory notes, an issuer writes an unlimited promise that he or she will pay a certain amount of money to the payee. This can be set up either on demand of the payee, or at a pre arranged future point in time. Specific terms are always arranged for the repayment of the debt in the promissory note.

Promissory notes are somewhat like IOU's and yet quite different. Unlike an IOU that only agrees that there is a debt in question, promissory notes are made up of a particular promise to pay the debt. In conversational vernacular, loan contract, loan agreement, or loan are often utilized in place of promissory note, even though such terms do not mean the same things legally. While a promissory note does provide proof of a loan in existence, it is not the loan contract. A loan contract instead has all of the conditions and terms of the particular loan arrangement within it.

Promissory notes contain a variety of term elements in them. Among these are the amount of principal, the rate of interest, the parties involved, the repayment terms, the date, and the date of maturity. From time to time, provisions may be included pertaining to the payee's rights should the issuer default. These rights could include the ability to foreclose on the issuer's assets.

A particular type of promissory note is a Demand Promissory note. This specific kind does not come with an exact date of maturity. Instead, it is due when the lender demands repayment. Generally, in these cases lenders only allow several days advance notice before the payment must be made.

Within the U.S., the Article 3 of the Uniform Commercial Code regulates most promissory notes. These negotiable forms of promissory notes are heavily used along with other documents in mortgages that involve financing purchases of real estate properties. When people make loans in between each other, the making and signing of promissory notes are commonly critical for the purposes of record keeping and paying taxes. Businesses also receive capital via the use of promissory notes that are sometimes referred to as commercial papers. These promissory notes became a finance source for the creditors of the firm receiving money.

Promissory notes have functioned like currency that proved to be privately issued in the past. Because of this, such promissory notes that are bearer negotiable have mostly been made illegal, since they represent an alternative to the officially sanctioned currency. Promissory notes go back to well before the 1500's in Western Europe. Tradition claims that the very first one ever signed existed in Milan in 1325. Reference is made to some being issued between Barcelona and Genoa back in 1384, even though we no longer have the promissory notes themselves. The first one that we still have dates back to 1553 where Ginaldo Giovanni Battista Stroxxi issued one that he created in Medina del Campo, Spain against the city of Besancon.

Refinance

When the word refinance is used, it is referring to the act of refinancing, or canceling out a currently existing debt with another debt that a bank or refinance company issues under alternative terms. By far and away the most popular refinancing that pertains to consumers is for mortgages on houses. Debt replacements that are performed in conditions of financial distress are also known as debt restructuring.

Home owners might choose to refinance their mortgage for a variety of reasons. It can assist them in meeting a range of end goals. You as a home owner might be interested in lowering your monthly payments on the mortgage through attaining a better interest rate or lengthening the terms of the loan.

You could lessen the amount of interest that you pay during the loan's term and expand the equity build up by going through a refinance to get a loan with a shorter life. You could also decrease your exposure to the risk of rising interest rates through obtaining a fixed term loan in place of a balloon mortgage or adjustable rate mortgage. Finally, you might be interested in drawing out home equity in order to do debt consolidation or to cover the costs of major expenses that you are encountering elsewhere.

The act of refinancing eliminates the original mortgage loan. This is then replaced with a new loan. There are many factors that you will have to decide in obtaining this new loan. This includes what type of loan is most ideal for the circumstances, which lender you will utilize, which term and rate are most advantageous, and the fees that you feel are reasonable. Because of these complicated decisions that must be made, consumers should seek out advice in their refinancing. If you do not possess a clear comprehension of all that is involved with the refinancing procedure, then you could accidentally put your house or your finances in danger.

There are risks associated with refinancing. These are principally penalty clauses that are also known as call provisions. When you pay off a mortgage loan early, these penalties would be triggered along with closing fees. The refinancing itself will entail transaction fees. All of these fees should be figured up and considered before you begin a project to refinance your home loan. This is especially the case since all of the fees together may eliminate any potential savings that you hoped to realize through the refinancing.

Another possible downside to refinancing loans is that they may provide you with lower payments every month on the same amount of money to be repaid. In this case, you will pay a greater amount of interest throughout the loan term. You would also pay on the debt for a great number of additional years over the original mortgage's terms. This is why it is so important to determine not only the upfront charges, but also the variable and ongoing costs involved in refinancing as a factor in the decision on whether to pursue it or not.

Rate of Return

In the worlds of finance and business, the rate of return, also known by its acronym ROR, proves to be the ratio of money lost or gained pertaining to an investment and the sum of money that is originally invested in it. This rate of return is also called the rate of profit or more commonly the return on investment, or ROI.

The sum of money that is lost or gained could be called the loss or profit, interest, or even net loss or net income. Regarding the money that is actually invested, it is sometimes called the capital, asset, or principle. It is also referred to as the cost basis of an investment. Rate of return or Return on Investment is commonly stated as a percentage and not a fraction.

This rate of return is one measurement of how much cash is made or lost as a direct result of the investment in question. It quantifies the amount of income stream or cash flow that moves from the investment itself to the investor as a percentage of the original amount that the investor put into the investment. Such cash flow that accrues to the investor comes in a number of forms. It might be interest, profit, capital gains and losses, or dividends received. These capital gains and losses happen as the investment's sale price is greater or less than its initial purchase price. The use of the term cash flow includes everything except for the return of the original invested money.

Rates of return can be figured up as averages covering a number of different time periods. They may also be determined for only one time frame. When these calculations are being made, it is important not to mix up annualized and annual rates of return. Annualized rates of return prove to be geometric average returns figured up over several or even numerous periods. Annualized returns might be the investment return on a period less than or greater than a year, for example for six months or three years. The rates of return are then multiplied out or divided in order to come up with a one year rate of return that can be compared against other annual rates of return. As an example, if an investment possessed a one percent rate of return per month, then this might be more appropriately expressed as an annualized rate of return of twelve percent. Or, if you had a three year rate of return amounting to fifteen percent, then you could say that this is a five percent annualized rate of return.

Annual rates of return are instead returns figured up for single time frame periods. These time frames are commonly one year periods running from the first of January to the last day of December. Alternatively, they could cover any year long period, regardless of what month and day they started and ended.

Residual

Residual refers to residual income. Residual income can have several different meanings depending on the context that you use. For an individual, residual income proves to be the money that remains at the end of a month after all financial responsibilities for the month are covered.

These include living costs, taxes, and housing costs. Where business is concerned, residual incomes are the operating income that is additional as compared to the typical minimum amount of operating assets that are controlled. Residual income furthermore refers to passive income that is earned. In this form of the term, it relates to all income that is created as a result of activities that are indirect. These might include royalties, rental income, investment portfolio returns, website revenues, or passively managed businesses, all of which qualify as residual income.

The word residual is a variation on the word residue. Residue means anything that stays behind because of some other substance or cause. So, residual income proves to be additional money made because of another activity like penning a novel and collecting royalties for the sale of every book.

Rental incomes are residual as they remain from the action of buying a house and then renting it to a tenant who pays you a monthly rental fee. Work is involved in this activity, although a property management company can do it on your behalf. The rewards for this rental project can be significant, as you enjoy the continuous rental stream as well as any increases in the value of the real estate property underlying it. Rental income can be utilized to pay for potentially an entire mortgage.

Income from investment portfolios is similarly considered to be residual income. Both dividends and interest are acquired as an additional, passive benefit of possessing stocks, bonds, mutual funds, and other instruments. This residual income is not guaranteed from these investments, but it is common for investors.

A form of residual income that is growing in popularity these days is website, or Internet based, revenues. Internet revenues are commonly those that you make from having advertising on a given website. The dollar value of the advertising is mostly based on the number of visitors to the page. A significant amount of start up work is required to create the website and get it highly ranked on the major search engines. After this, you can see continuous monthly profits that you earn as a result of the advertising, which builds up a residual income. This amount of money could be as little as a few dollars a month to possibly thousands of dollars per month.

A last form of residual income can result from a business. If your company becomes large enough, you may be able to hire a manager to run it. The income that supports you while the manager runs the business is then considered residual income.

Revenue

Revenue refers to the amount of money which firms generate in receivables within a certain time frame. It includes deductions for merchandise which is returned as well as any applicable discounts. This is also known as the gross income or sometimes the "top line" amount. Net income can be figured out by subtracting the costs from the revenue.

Analysts and accountants determine the amount of revenue simply by taking the price for which services and goods sell and multiplying this by the quantity of units or the actual amount which the firm sells. Sometimes revenue is referred to as "REVs."

There are a number of other definitions and synonyms for revenues. Some call it sales in layman's terms. Whatever name businesses and individuals refer to it by, revenue proves to be the total amount of cash which a company garners through its aggregate business activities. The price to sales ratio is one measurement in business that relies on revenues for the denominator. This contrasts with the competing measurement of price to earnings ratio, which utilizes the profits instead for its denominator.

Revenue can be figured up by several different means. It is really up to the method of accounting which companies and corporations choose to employ. With accrual accounting, sales which the firm makes using credit also count among the revenues so long as the customers have taken delivery of the services or goods. This is why investors and analysts must review the company's cash flow statement in order to evaluate how effectively a firm actually collects on the money which its customers owe it.

The other primary form of determining a company's revenues is through cash accounting. This form of accounting utilizes only sales for the revenues' quotient once the money a customer owes has been collected by the firm in question. When a customer gives the money to a corporation or company, the firm recognizes it as a receipt instead of the general category of revenues. Companies can actually have receipts that do not include revenues. This is possible if a customer were to pay for a service in advance of receiving it or for purchased goods which they have not yet received.

Revenue can also be called "top line" since income statements display them first on the report. Analysts then take revenues and deduct the expenses so that they can come up with the "bottom line," which is also called simply profit or alternatively net income.

Many times investors evaluate both a firm's net income and revenues independently of one another so that they can ascertain how strong a business' health really turns out to be. The reason for this is that net income can increase while revenues remain flat. Cost cutting can actually cause this phenomenon. This scenario is not a positive sign for the longer term growth potential for a firm.

Analysts and investors often further subdivide the revenues from a given company or corporation according to the groups which generate the money. Company accountants can also divide up the receipts of the firm into several categories of operating revenues, the core business of the firm's sales, and non-operating revenues that come from secondary sources. Such non-operating variants are typically not recurring or can not be forecast successfully. This is why these are sometimes known as one-time gains or events. Examples of this could be money gained through lawsuits, investment windfalls, or receipts from selling an asset.

Where a government is concerned, revenue refers to the receipts they obtain as a result of fees, taxation, fines, securities sales, transfers, intergovernmental grants, resource rights and mineral rights, or any sales of government assets or state-owned and -run companies which they might make.

In the world of not for profit organizations, such revenues are commonly referred to by the phrase of "gross receipts." Among the components that make up these receipts are donations from companies, foundations, and individuals; investment returns; grants out of governmental agencies and entities; membership dues and fees; and fundraising endeavors.

Reverse Mortgages

Reverse mortgages are special types of loans. They are limited to homeowners who are at least 62 years old. These mortgages permit the owners to take a portion of their home equity and convert it to cash. The seniors may use these mortgage proceeds in any way that they like.

The government came up with these unique products because they were looking for a way to help out retired individuals who did not have enough income. The idea was that they might unlock the wealth they had built up in their houses to provide for health care, outside home care, or ordinary monthly costs of living.

These loans are referred to as reverse mortgages because the home owners do not send a lender monthly payments. These are the opposite of traditional mortgages. Lenders provide the borrower with payments instead. The home owners have several advantages. They do not have to repay the loan until they either no longer live in the home or sell it. They also do not make any regular monthly payments against the balance of the loan. The borrowers are required to keep up with their homeowners insurance, property taxes, and any association or homeowner fees.

The most common type of reverse mortgages are known as HECM Home Equity Conversion Mortgages. The U.S. HUD Housing and Urban Development designed and oversees these. These are not loans from the government. Rather they are mortgage loans that lenders provide with insurance from the FHA Federal Housing Administration. In these particular types, borrowers accrue a 1.25% insurance fee as part of the balance on the loan. This increases the loan balance annually.

This insurance is useful for two protections. In case the lender can not make the monthly payment, it provides for it. Should the house resale value be insufficient to pay back the final loan balance at the end, it makes the lender whole. The government and its insurance fund would then clear any balance that remained.

These HECMs comprise the majority of such reverse mortgages in the United States. Included in their regulations is that the senior borrowers must undergo third party counseling to help them with all of the documents and agreements.

The other type of reverse mortgage is a Proprietary Reverse Mortgage. The mortgage lenders that provide these also insure them privately. This means that they do not have to follow the regulations as with the HECMs. The majority of firms that offer these mortgages choose to honor the identical consumer protections featured in the HECM program. This means that mandatory counseling is usually a part of their programs.

These types are also known as jumbo reverse mortgages. Seniors with larger value houses go with these kinds since there is a $625,500 maximum loan limit on the government's HECMs. Two companies in the country presently offer these types of PRMs. These are the Orange, California based American Advisors Group and the Tulsa, Oklahoma based America Reverse Mortgage.

Regardless of the type of reverse mortgage, the lenders have to put potential borrowers through a financial assessment before making the loan. This is so that they can be certain the seniors will be able to pay the future homeowners insurance and taxes and afford to live in the house for the loan's life. To do this, lenders consider all of the income streams of the borrower. This includes their Social Security, investments, and any pensions. The home owners are also required to give the lender their tax returns and bank statements so that expenses and income may be properly documented.

Royalties

Royalties are payments which owners receive in exchange for the use of their property. This most typically covers natural resources, franchises, patents, and copyrighted works. Royalty payments go to the property in question's legal owner. Individuals who want to utilize the owners' patents, property, franchise, natural resources, or copyrighted works will do so with the intention of creating a revenue stream or realizing a lump sum income. Royalties are typically intended to provide compensation for the licensing of the asset. As such, these arrangements become legally binding.

Much of the time, these royalties are stated in percentage of revenue terms. They can also be arranged to fit a particular scenario or environment. They are often employed as the vehicle for realizing income in instances where the owner, inventor, or natural resource holder wishes to sell the product in question in exchange for payments against future revenues that this activity might create for the third party licensor.

An example of this is Microsoft. The computer software giant earns a royalty from every installation of the internationally standard Windows operating system on almost any computer a manufacturer produces. Such an example relates to creative content, copyrights, and patents.

A royalty could also apply to resources, trade marks, art works, books and published works, copyright materials, franchises, patents, and resource holdings. Even fashion designers are able to charge a royalty to other companies that wish to make use of their designs or names. Authors, production pros, and musical artists also receive this kind of compensation when a firm or individual uses their copyrighted and produced works. Cable and satellite firms pay a royalty to the owner of a television channel so they can offer the most stations in a country.

The oil and gas business is one that is rife with royalties. Companies provide a royalty to a landowner in exchange for permission to gather the natural resources off of their private property. This might amount to so much money per barrel of oil or per cubic foot of natural gas which they extract.

A license agreement is a key component of a royalty. It represents the terms by which the property owner will receive the payments. This clearly and legally explains the restrictions and limitations of the royalty in question. As an example, it would deal with the length of time the agreement will endure, the geographic territorial limitations, and the specific amounts they will pay for the various kinds of products utilized or extracted. These types of license agreements are differently and specifically regulated depending on whether the owner of the resource or property in question is a private individual or the government.

A royalty rate represents the specific amount of payment that must be paid for a given service or product. This will naturally depend on the kind of fee the third party is providing. There are a number of different factors involved in a royalty rate. Among the most frequently cited examples are alternative option availability, rights' exclusivity, the relevant risks involved, technological sustainability, structure of the market demand, and scope of the innovation which the service or product offers.

These terms should not be confused with a royalty trust unit. Such units provide the holder of the unit with a share of the income which the properties a trust owns actually produce. These royalty trusts acquire ownership stakes in cash flows or general operating concerns. The royalty trust itself will own the cash flow or income which the company is generating. They will then pass through this money to the trust royalty unit holders. Such royalty units have often been viewed as positive and desirable investments since the income which the asset creates only becomes subject to individual tax levels. There is no so-called "double taxation" as common stocks dividends experience (on both the company earning the money and then the person receiving it again).

S Corporation

S Corporation refers to the Subchapter S Corporation type of company filing which measures up to certain requirements set by the IRS Internal Revenue Service. This status provides a corporation which possesses a hundred or fewer shareholders all of the advantages of incorporation while also keeping the benefits of only being tax treated like a partnership.

One of the many benefits to this type of incorporation is that it is able to pass all of the company income straight through to the shareholders, thus avoiding the problems of double taxation which are a real issue with shareholders of public companies. There are some particular requirements that must be met to enjoy these advantages. The firm must be domiciled as a domestic corporation. It cannot possess over a hundred shareholders, and it may only count a single class of stock.

Such S Corporations can pass all of their credits, deductions, losses, and any income straight through to the various shareholders. They may then report this loss or income directly via their own personal tax returns. It allows them to pay out their taxes at generally considerably lower individual income tax rates. There are some built in gains on which the S Corporation will pay the taxes at the corporate level, but these are few and far between.

These S Corporations have to be domestically headquartered firms whose shareholders are estates, certain kinds of trusts, and individuals. A corporation, partnership, or non-resident alien can never qualify for this category of shareholder. There are also some financial institutions, domestic international sales firms, and insurance outfits that are not allowed to incorporate as an S Corporation.

There are some significant advantages to establishing an S Corporation. It builds up real creatibility with employees, possible customers, investors, and suppliers as it proves the owner is seriously committed to the firm. Employees may also be shareholders in the company, which allows them to enjoy company salaries while also receiving any corporate dividends and distributions which are tax-free as compared to the investment in the company. This is certainly beneficial for morale.

Paying out distributions in the form of dividends or salaries allows the owners to lower the self-employment tax liability at the same time as it creates wage and expense deductions for the firm. Since this S Corporation will not pay any federal taxes at company level, such losses can be utilized to offset other forms of income for the tax returns of the shareholders. It is always helpful to save money on the onerous American corporate income taxes, particularly for new firms. It is another benefit to these companies that the various interests within the corporation can be easily transferred without creating tax liability events and consequences. Complicated accounting rules do not create restrictions nor does the company have to adjust the basis of property either.

Yet there are also a few downsides to establishing a company as an S Corporation. The IRS closely examines any and all distribution payments made to shareholders in the forms of either dividends or salaries to make sure that they are really employees working in the firm. If wages become characterized as dividends, then the company will lose its compensation paid deduction. Should dividends be characterized as wages, then the company will pay a greater amount of employment taxes. It is also easy for mistakes to be made in the areas of notification, consent, election, filing requirements, or stock ownership requirements that lead to the S Corporation being untimely terminated. There is considerable money and time investment in such a corporate structuring as well.

The owner will have to begin by filling in and filing articles of incorporation to the Secretary of State, get a registered agent on board for the company, and pay any relevant fees and costs involved. Owners often have to pay yearly reporting fees and franchise taxes along with ongoing types of fees. These may be inexpensive, but they can still be deducted under the cost of doing business category. Even if the investors possess non-voting shares of stock in this form of corporate structuring, they will still get distribution and dividend rights.

Sales Tax

Sales Tax refers to a government imposed tax on consumption of both services and goods. Traditional sales taxes are collected at the appropriate points of sale. The retailers gather the money which they then pass on to the appropriate governmental agency. Businesses are also liable to pay such sales taxes to the relevant jurisdiction (state or local government) if they have what is known as a nexus in that jurisdiction. This could be an employee, physical office location, presence of some other type, or an affiliate. The laws of the jurisdiction in question determine which of these criteria apply in determining business residence.

Conventional forms of sales taxes only become charged to or are payable by the final seller of a service or a good. Since the overwhelming numbers of goods in today's economies go through a range of manufacturing points and stages, they become a part and parcel of many different entities' operations. This means that great quantities of paper work must be kept and filed in order to determine the end seller who will be finally liable for the sales taxes owed.

As an example to better understand the dilemma this poses, consider a sheep farmer. The farmer sells his wool to a firm which makes yarn. The yarn maker would be responsible for the sales tax unless it is able to gain a resale certificate from the responsible governmental agency. This certificate must declare that the yarn maker is not the final user. Next, the yarn maker will sell its yarn products to a clothing manufacturer. This manufacturer also has to get such a resale certificate. The clothing maker then sells its wooly sweater to an outlet store. It is this outlet store that must charge sales tax to its customers besides the price of the sweater.

The various jurisdictions all charge their own sales tax rates. This can be confusing as they are also overlapping on one another. In some localities, the state, the county, and even the municipality (city or town) will all levy their individual sales tax amounts.

The nexus point raises an often-confusing set of issues for many businesses. They are only resident to a particular jurisdiction (state or locality) if the government there defines the nexus in a way that will call them resident for business purposes. Such a nexus is defined usually by the criteria of physical presence. Such a presence may not only be limited to maintaining a warehouse, factory, or office though.

It could mean that a company which has an employee who lives in the state will be considered to have a nexus. Partner websites (which direct traffic over to a business' websites in exchange for cash payments), or affiliates, can also be considered to be part of a nexus. This illustrates the difficulties encountered between sales tax collection and the sprawling and growing arena of e-commerce. Bigger states like New York have enacted what they call "Amazon laws." These make all internet retailers selling goods to customers in their states pay the sales tax, regardless of whether or not they maintain a physical presence in the state. The laws were named for the giant Internet retailers like Amazon.com.

Sales taxes usually work on a percentage basis of the goods' prices. As an example, states could collect a five percent sales tax, while the county gets two percent, and the city one percent. This would mean the residents in that given city of the county would have to pay a total sales tax of eight percent.

Many necessary items can be exempt from these taxes to help the lower income earners. This includes food as well as sometimes clothing items which cost under $200 in total. Other taxes specially levied on only certain products are called excise taxes. Many of these the states refer to as "sin taxes." In essence, this kind of excise tax would cover cigarettes and alcohol, which have been historically labeled by the churches as sins. New York State levies a $4.35 excise (and "sin") tax on every pack of cigarettes, as of 2016.

Securities

Securities refer to financial instruments which stand for a position of ownership in a corporation which is publically traded. These would be stock shares. They could also be a creditor-like relationship to a corporation or a government entity or agency. This security would be called a bond. They might also be an option, which is the right but not obligation to acquire and own something. A security is ultimately a financial instrument that an investor or company can sell or transfer and which represents a kind of financial holding and value. The entity or corporation which provides the security to the investors is called the issuer.

There are two principal types of securities, equities and debts. Equities refer to shareholder-held ownership of a corporation. A stock is the most common example of these equities. Equity holders may receive dividends and sell their position to another party for a capital gain when the price increases to higher than they that for which they purchased it originally.

Debt securities are proof of creditor-borrower arrangements. These stand for money which a corporation or government agency borrows and which they must repay to the creditor. The debt security has terms which outline and specify the cash amount that they have borrowed, the maturity or renewal date, and the interest rate that applies. There are many forms of these debt instruments. The most common include CDs certificates of deposit, preferred stocks, corporate and government bonds, and CMOs or CDOs which are Collateralized Mortgage Obligations or Collateralized Debt Obligations.

Besides the standard forms of debt and equity types, there are also hybrid securities. They merge features of an equity and debt security together. Equity warrants are classic examples of this type of security. These are options that a company issues which provide its holders with the ability to buy stock shares in a given time frame for a pre-determined price. Convertibles are bonds which may be transferred into stock shares of common stock in the company which issues them. Preferred shares are actual shares of stock that pay dividends or interest ahead of the common stock class of shares.

Two main organizations regulate the issuance and sale of such a security within the United States. These are the SEC Securities and Exchange Commission and the FINRA Financial Industry Regulatory Authority.

Issuers of a security like this could be one of several different types of organizations. Municipal governments can issue bonds in order to raise specific project funding. Buyers of a security might be retail investors who purchase and sell them for their own accounts. Wholesale investors are those which trade the security as a financial institution working at the instruction for their customers and clients. There are also institutional investors which are a major category of security buyers. These include insurance companies, managed funds, pension funds, and investment banks like Goldman Sachs.

The purpose of a security is to float a debt or ownership instrument so that a commercial enterprise or government agency can raise fresh capital. By selling such a security, corporations are able to create money for business purposes and acquisitions. Sometimes the demand in the market place is strong enough and the pricing arrangements are favorable enough that it makes more sense for companies to issue securities to raise money rather than choose to borrow them in the form of loans or bonds. Government entities can not issue and float stock. Instead they may only issue debt in the form of general obligation or specific revenue bonds.

Securities which companies issue in the primary market they do in the form of an IPO initial public offering. Once these shares are floated and sold, all issued shares of stock are called secondary offerings. This is the case even when they still sell them in the primary market. Companies can also privately place such securities. There are cases where both private placement and public primary market floating takes place. The secondary market is the place where such a security becomes transferred from one investor to a different investor.

Shareholders

Shareholders are companies, people, or institutions which own minimally a single share of the stock in a given company. They can also be referred to as stockholders. These stockholders are not only investors, but also the owners of the corporation. As owners, they gain the advantageous results from the firm's success. This can translate into higher stock prices, dividend payouts, or hopefully both. Should the corporation not perform well, the stock holders can similarly lose value in their investments as the stock price goes down.

There is a difference between shareholders and owners of partnerships and sole proprietorships. The stakeholders in corporations do not experience personal liability for the financial and debt obligations of the corporation. Should the company in question fail, creditors can not attempt to secure payments or assets from the stockholders as they might be able to do from owners of entities which are privately held.

Corporations with shareholders have another important difference from other structures of businesses. They depend on their executive management and board of directors to handle the day to day operations. This means that the stock holders do not have much control over the daily operations of the company.

Shareholders may not have much involvement in the company's decisions, but they still have important rights. These are specified by the corporation's bylaws and charter. One of these is the right to go through the company records and financial books. Another is to sue the company for officer and director committed mistakes. Even common stock holders have the right to vote on important corporate decisions like whether to agree to a potential merger or on the makeup of the board of directors.

Shareholders have what may be their most important right when a company goes into liquidation through dissolution or bankruptcy. They have the rights to regain a representative amount of the recovered proceeds. They are in line after the secured debt holders including bondholders, preferred stock holders, and creditors, all of whom have precedence over the common stockholders.

Stock holders have several other rights which they enjoy. They receive a part of dividends which their company announces. They also gain the privilege to attend in person the annual meeting of the corporation. Here they are able to learn more regarding the performance of the firm. They can also choose to sit in on the meeting using a conference call. If these common stock holders are not able to or interested in going to the annual meeting, they can instead choose to vote through the mail or online using a vote by proxy. All of these rights which belong to preferred and common shareholders are detailed in the corporate governance policy.

A great number of corporations elect to create two classes of stock. These are common and preferred shares. The majority of stock holders purchase and hold common stocks since they are more of them and they are less expensive than preferred shares. Unlike preferred stock holders who are due to receive dividends every quarter, common shareholders must wait on the board of directors to decide if and when they will be paid a dividend in a given quarter. The directors must decide if this is an appropriate way to utilize the corporation's funds.

Preferred stockholders lack the voting rights of common shareholders. They do receive higher dividends on a more frequent basis. Their payments have to be paid at least yearly and their dividends are also guaranteed. For investors more interested in creating a reliable annual income from investments, preferred shares can be a very helpful tool.

Stagflation

Stagflation refers to the simultaneous problems of high unemployment, stagnated economic growth, and persistently high inflation. It is an unlikely scenario, as slowing economies typically reduce demand sufficiently in order to keep higher prices in check. When workers lose their jobs, they purchase less. Businesses are then usually forced to reduce their prices in order to convince remaining customers to buy. It is this typically slower growth in market economies that prevents inflation from running away.

Stagflation policies typically lead to hyperinflation. Central banks that expand the country's money supply as the national supply is restricted do so by printing up additional currency. Monetary policies then create additional credit. This increases demand from consumers. It is the simultaneous supply restrictions that keep companies from producing enough to keep up with the rising demand.

Such a scenario happened in Zimbabwe back in 2004. Their government printed up so much currency that it pushed well beyond stagflation and evolved into ruinous hyperinflation. A stagflation in the United States only transpired in the 1970s. At the time the U.S. government expanded its dollars significantly to try to create additional economic growth. While they did this, President Nixon's wage price controls severely limited business-produced supplies.

The name stagflation actually comes from the 1973 to 1975 era recession. In those six consecutive quarters, the U.S. GDP shrank in size. Inflation literally tripled in 1973 alone, jumping from a relatively tame 3.4% to 9.6%. In the time between February of 1974 and April of 1975, inflation stubbornly remained between 10% and 12%.

Experts today look back at the 1973 Arab-led oil embargo as the crisis that triggered first oil price inflation. At this time, OPEC nations drastically cut their oil exports to the United States, forcing prices to quadruple. The inflation from oil spread to many other parts of the economy dependent on oil and gasoline, such as shipping, rail, and trucking.

The mild recession of 1970 was the precursor to the problems. President

Richard Nixon in his bid to be re-elected introduced as series of four fiscal and monetary economic policies that helped to ensure he won. These unfortunately also created the conditions for stagflation a few years later.

Nixon's first mistake was the start of wage and price controls. U.S. businesses were unable to raise their final prices even as import costs were soaring. They could only respond by reducing costs via worker layoffs. That boosted unemployment and further slowed economic growth by lowering demand. Nixon secondly took the U.S. off the gold standard to stop an international run on American gold reserves. This only crushed the value of the dollar and created still higher import prices and yet more inflation.

In order to fight off the inflation, the Federal Reserve had no choice but to continue raising interest rates. These reached their peak of 20% by 1979. Because the Fed did this in an up and down motion, businesses became confused and chose to keep up higher prices.

Though stagflation has not yet reoccurred in the U.S., Americans became worried it might again in 2011. The Fed had begun employing aggressive expansive monetary policies to save the U.S. economy from the grips of the 2008 financial crisis and Great Recession. This caused many to fear that high inflation would return. The economy only grew at low levels form 1% to 2% at this time.

Economists observed stagflation was a viable risk if inflation rose while the economy continued to struggle. Instead, deflation became the serious concern of the day. Massive increases in global liquidity were used to try to fight off this opposite kind of problem.

Stocks

Stocks are financial instruments that are issued by publicly traded corporations. These shares of stocks prove to be the tiniest portion of ownership that you can acquire in a company. Even by owning a single share of a company's stock you are a small part owner of the firm.

Owning shares of stock gives you the privilege of voting for the underlying company's board of directors, along with other critical issues that the company is considering. Should a company decide to distribute earnings to share holders as dividends, then you will get a portion of them.

With the ownership of stock, your liability in the company is only limited to the value of your shares. This means that should a company lose a lawsuit and be forced to pay an enormous fine or judgment, then you can not be made to contribute to it. The company's creditors also can not pursue you if the company runs into financial trouble and goes bankrupt.

Two different types of stock shares exist. These are common shares and preferred shares. The vast majority of shares that are issued are common stock shares. These are the shares that members of the public hold most of the time. They come with full voting rights and also the possibility of receiving dividends that the company pays out.

Preferred stocks come with fewer voting rights but give preferential treatment for dividend payment. Preferred stock issues are paid out before common share dividends. Companies that offer preferred stock typically pay dividends on both classes of shares anyway. Preferred stocks also have a higher claim on the assets of a company if it fails.

Liquidity is a feature of stocks that should always be considered. Common stock shares are almost always more liquid than are preferred shares. Large companies offer the greatest amount of liquidity in the trading of their stocks. Because of the depth of the stock markets, you are able to purchase and sell the shares of practically all companies that are publicly traded at any time that the exchanges are working.

When you purchase a stock, you are looking for two different kinds of gains.

Cash flow or passive income with stocks comes from the dividends that they declare and pay out. Capital gains appreciation is realized when you buy a stock at a lower price than the price that you get when you later sell it. While cash flow dividends are smaller payments that are realized on a generally quarterly basis, capital gains turn out to be larger one time returns made when you sell the underlying stock shares investment. At this point, you would no longer own the stock and you would have to purchase another stock in order to work towards cash flow gains from dividends, as well as other possible capital gains.

Subsidies

Subsidies are types of financial support or aid which a government or organization extends out to an economic industry, institution, individual, or business. These are done for the purpose of fostering particular economic or even social policies. The government is the most common provider of this type of assistance, but such support can also come from Non Governmental Organizations.

Such grants can be derived from a number of different forms of aid. These include indirect help as with insurance, tax breaks, accelerated depreciation, lower interest loans, and rent rebates. They can also be direct assistance in the form of interest-free loans or outright grants of cash or other assets. The ultimate goal of such a subsidy is to alleviate a form of financial burden. They are often deemed to be to the overall advantage of the entire public and not a specific person, business, or interest group by the very nature of the group receiving the help.

Such a subsidy grant is often regarded by governments as privileges. This is because they help with a relevant burden which was somehow unfairly levied on the receiver. They could also encourage a certain behavior or ultimate result through delivering financial support, as with farming subsidies to encourage domestic agriculture.

In general, such a subsidy will typically benefit a segment of an industry within a national economy. These can be employed to help out markets which are suffering by reducing perceived burdens from which they struggle. They might also boost additional development within an industry or research line via offering financial support for the efforts and work. Many times, these areas of production or research do not receive the necessary assistance which they require from the workings of the mainstream economy. Sometimes they are even outright disadvantaged by the actions undertaken by rival economies and nations.

There are two principal forms of subsidy aid as mentioned previously. These are direct and indirect subsidies. The direct form encompasses payments specifically directed to a certain industry or a given group. Cash is usually the medium of exchange offered to the receiving parties.

With indirect forms of a subsidy, there is no preset monetary value at which the help is limited or specified when it is provided to the individual, businesses, or industry. This might involve special goods or services which are price reduced. It could also include another form of government support to the given industry. It helps the much needed items to be bought at under the present market cost. This level of savings can vary greatly depending on the amount of the given organizations' participation in the program.

Governments, in particular the American Federal and European Union governments, provide many different types of subsidies. These are not only limited to help for domestic industry or farmers. They can also involve welfare and social assistance as with payments, student loans, grants, housing loans, and a farm subsidy. When domestic farming struggles to endure within the intensely competitive international farming arena because of their lower prices of other countries' farms, the U.S. or EU government bodies may provide actual cash subsidies to the farmers in order for them to afford to sell their products at the lower market rates. The intended goal is that they will still reap financial rewards sufficient to justify continuing to farm with this outright monetary assistance.

More recently, the government has become involved with health care subsidy to private citizens on an individual and family level. The Affordable Care Act of the U.S. allows its citizens to receive subsidies dependent on their size and income of the relevant household. Such a subsidy is intended to reduce the enormous out of pocket expenses associated with high health care premiums and co-payments for households which earn under a minimum income threshold. The funds of the subsidies go directly to the insurance company in question. This reduces the amount of money which the insurance company requires from the individual or household.

Tax Refund

A Tax Refund refers to money which the IRS Internal Revenue Service gives back to a tax payer for overpayment of their taxes in a given tax year. For the eight out of ten Americans who receive them most every year, they evoke feelings of wild celebration. The truth of the matter is it simply means that this majority overpaid their income tax out of their payroll tax withholding with their employer throughout the calendar year. This is not a good thing in reality.

Self-employed people will also receive a refund if they have overpaid their estimated taxes. This does not represent free money or additional income when a tax check arrives in the mail or is alternatively direct deposited. Instead, it signifies that the recipient cheerfully agreed to loan Uncle Sam money without charging him any interest for the service.

It is also possible for tax refunds to be issued out of refundable tax credits. This can occur if any money remains from such credits after the taxes due from the federal income have been covered. After the federal government receives and processes all of the return for the tax year in question, it must formally sign off on a refund before the money will be dispatched.

The amount of time that this requires varies according to the means which individuals employ in filing their taxes. Electronically filed taxes-refund processing times are usually sent in under 21 days from the Internal Revenue Service accepting the return. It is possible for delays to hinder this by as much as 12 weeks, though it is highly unlikely that this would happen. Paper tax returns which are mailed typically take from six to eight weeks to be issued and arrive in the mail in the form of a traditional paper check.

If individuals wait until peak tax return season to file, their refunds will commonly be delayed. Tax preparers at the IRS can and do become overwhelmed as easily as any person at this busy time of the year. After all, the IRS is not guaranteeing the time frame for the refunds to be sent out, only estimating their best guess. This is why those waiting for a tax refund should never wait on such a payout to fund a critical purchase or make a time sensitive payment (on a house, mortgage, or other credit card bill).

For those who do find themselves in desperate straits to receive such a refund though, there are loans against imminent refunds which taxpayers can apply for and receive. Some tax preparers, such as H&R Block, will issue refunds against owed refunds as well, in exchange for a small percentage convenience fee. All delay liabilities then transfer to the tax preparing firm and away from the individual tax filer.

Where electronic tax refunds are concerned, individuals have three choices. They can have the IRS deposit them to a checking account, savings account, or retirement account (such as an IRA). Besides this, one could have the IRS purchase a $5,000 or less Series I savings bond if he or she fancies receiving less than a single measly one percent per year in interest.

People have up to three years from the point of filing to claim their refund. This means that now in 2017, filers could still apply for a refund from the tax year 2014. When the IRS grants an extension for any reason, the deadline for the three years starts at the end of the deadline extension.

The sad news is that sometimes people are not allowed to keep their whole refund. The IRS could make a tragic mistake and overpay a refund. They will get this back eventually one way or the other. Any individuals who owe back payments on child support will also have this seized, as they would for back taxes of overdue student loan bills. It is also possible to get a smaller than expected check. In the event that the remaining money does not show up within two weeks of the incorrect amount, it is always a recommended idea to contact the Internal Revenue Service directly.

Trader

Trader describes any person who participates in selling and buying financial assets on any of the global financial markets. These individuals might do this on their own behalf or instead on that of an institution or another individual. Some people have the tendency to confuse the titles trader and investor. The primary difference between the two pertains to the amount of time that each type of individual holds on to the asset in question. Traders generally keep assets for much shorter time frames in an effort to take advantage of rapidly developing trends. Investors on the other hand usually possess a longer time frame horizon for investing.

Such a trader might work on behalf of a financial institution. When this is the case, he or she will trade utilizing the firm's credit and money. The person is then typically a salaried employee who has the opportunity to earn bonuses which are based on performance and returns garnered for the employing firm. Many other traders are self-employed. In these scenarios, they use their own money and credit to trade and also get to keep any and all of the profits personally.

There are definite disadvantages to trading shorter term. Among these are the spread between bids and ask that must be paid each time both in and out of the instrument and also the commission fees. This is how traders are able to run up substantial commission costs, as they often pursue such short term trading strategies in and out of financial instruments in an effort to realize profits. Thanks to the growing quantities of extremely competitive discount brokerage firms (like TD Ameritrade, E*TRADE, and Interactive Brokers), commission fees have become less of a disadvantage. With the advent of the all-electronic trading platforms offered (such as Meta Trader 4), foreign exchange market spreads have tightened considerably.

Still, the tax situation in the United States disadvantages traders and short term speculators on purpose. The Internal Revenue Service in America assesses steeply higher capital gains taxes on what they consider to be short term capital gains. Traders pay taxes on this money as if the gains were ordinary income, while longer term capital gains assess at a flat 20 percent rate.

With the institutions, they often fit out and maintain dedicated trading rooms to provide a work space for their proprietary traders to purchase and sell huge varieties of financial products for their companies. In these interesting scenarios, every trader receives a specified and pre-determined limit for how big their positions can be, how great a loss they are allowed to accrue before the positions will be force closed out, and the maximum amount of maturity time on the given positions. Because these institutional trading firms run all of the associated trading risk, they have the privilege of keeping the majority of any and all of the profits. The traders are engaging in this activity as employees who work for a salary and potential bonuses for a job well done.

The vast majority of individuals instead trading for their own personal accounts do this either from a small office or from the convenience of their own home. They will choose to work with electronic trading platforms (whenever possible) provided through a competitive discount broker in order to keep trading costs as low and reasonable as possible.

The advantage to the discount brokers is that they assess far lower commission fees per transaction. The disadvantage which is the flip side of this coin is that they do not offer financial advice, or they instead provide a bare minimum amount of it. A great number of the discount brokers do provide margin trading accounts to their members. This helps the traders to quickly and effectively borrow money off of the broker (without having to provide advance notice of a trade) in order to engage in a larger purchase. While this boosts the position sizes they can afford, it also multiplies the potential for losses at the same time.

Transfer of Interest

A Transfer of Interest refers to an individual, business, or other organization choosing to transfer over its ownership in an asset or object. This could be a business entity, piece of Real Estate, or asset that the owner shifts to another party. Most commonly the term becomes utilized regarding the transferring of an entity's ownership of an interest in a business. This could involve transfers between parties in a limited liability company, a partnership, a privately held sole proprietorship, or even a corporation. In the vast majority of cases, such a transfer occurs with a contract known as a transfer of interest agreement.

In theory, any time individuals or businesses engage in a purchase, they are becoming party to a contract. Such contracts are actually making a Transfer of Interest in some form of real property in the vast majority of cases. As a concrete example, when an individual buys food off of a supermarket or produce stand, this literally represents an implied contract (evidenced by a receipt as proof of purchase). The end result is that the buyer becomes the transferring new owner of the food purchase. The same is true when people buy clothing from a department store. The ownership of the clothes becomes officially transferred by the contract which the store makes with the buyer when money changes hands in exchange for a receipt and the articles of clothing.

Any type of Transfer of Interest is affected with whatever terms the two parties agree upon at the time of transfer. These could involve legal restrictions and stipulations on the kind of interest which they will transfer between them. The appropriate agreement only has to state clearly the interest which will be transferred, the parties who are involved, and the sum being delivered in consideration of the interest transfer. After the transaction intent is clearly stated by the actions and/or verbal promises of the two parties in question, the agreement will be officially concluded so that the transfer becomes finalized.

Naturally the universe of Real Estate has its own highly evolved and carefully developed procedures for such an important Transfer of Interest. They commonly call this an assessable transfer of interest. It refers to the reality of taxation which goes along with tangible interest in and de facto ownership of Real Estate. These transfers mandate that the property will be appraised and fully re-evaluated in the tax year that follows the transfer. All transfers of Real Estate done either with a contract, trust, or deed will be treated as such by the taxing authorities in the relevant jurisdiction. Leases that last for more than 20 years also come under this requirement. The reason for such an evaluation of the property value is to be certain that the taxes are fairly and fully assessed on the Real Estate involved in the contractual transfer transaction.

It is many times the same when there is a Transfer of Interest in a business accomplished through a sale. This event often produces an assessable event which will require a tax assessment to be done. When the business is at least 50 percent sold, this will commonly be required. When a business is instead forfeited or foreclosed on and the change of status does not lead to an income tax event, then this is an exception to the tax assessment rule.

When a transfer occurs among an affiliated group's members, this is also an applicable exception to the assessment case. There are often these substantial tax ramifications to such a transfer of a business that the government will usually require that the business value be reassessed following the execution of the business transfer transaction in question.

Treasuries

Treasuries refer to United States Treasury Securities. These Treasuries are United States government debt that is actually issued and sold by the Department of the Treasury via the Bureau of Public Debt. The U.S. government uses its Treasury securities to finance the enormous and rising debt of the Federal government. In common and investor vernacular, these treasury securities are commonly simply called Treasuries.

Four different kinds of treasury securities exist. These are Treasury notes, Treasury bills, Treasury bonds, and TIPS, or Treasury Inflation Protected Securities. Other types of treasury securities are not marketed. These are comprised of savings bonds, Government Account Series debt given to trust funds that the government manages, and SLGS, or State and Local Government Series. The former marketable Treasury securities prove to be extremely liquid and also are traded significantly on the secondary market. The latter mentioned non marketable Treasury securities are only sold to subscribers. They may not be transferred back and forth via market sales.

The vast majority of U.S. Treasuries are actually held by other countries. As of January 2010, the top five largest holders of American Treasuries turn out to be China with $889 billion, Japan with $765.4 billion, the combined oil exporting nations with $218.4 billion, the United Kingdom with $206 billion, and Brazil with $169.1 billion. China and Japan combined hold an enormous $1.6 trillion worth of U.S. Treasuries.

These and other foreign countries have become such a large component of U.S. Treasuries debt purchases that many economists have grown afraid. They fear that since foreign nations now account for such a great percentage of U.S. Treasuries that should they decide to stop purchasing them, the U.S. debt and economy might simply collapse. The possibility that this is true has caused many observers to believe that the two economies of the United States and China are inextricably linked. Both countries are afraid of what would happen if the Chinese slowed their purchases of U.S. Treasuries. When Hillary Clinton, the U.S. Secretary of State, visited China earlier in 2010, she insisted that Beijing monetary authorities keep buying United States Treasuries. Her argument centered on the hope that this will pump the American economy back up, which would stimulate Chinese goods' imports back home.

China has demonstrated its frustration over the possible decline in value of its U.S. Treasuries holdings too. The Chinese Premier Wen Jia Bao has expressed concern and a warning that the Chinese holdings of U.S. Treasuries could be downgraded and devalued if Washington can not get its runaway debt under controlled.

Trust

A Trust proves to be a special type of fiduciary arrangement where one participant the trustor grants the other participant the trustee the rights to possess the property title or assets title for the advantages of the beneficiary, often times a third party. When it is utilized in the world of finance, this similarly refers to a kind of closed end investment fund collectively established as a public limited company.

Settlors ultimately establish such trusts. They elect to shift over all or a portion of their possessions (assets) to the trustees of the trust in this action. It is the trustees who ultimately maintain the assets on behalf of the beneficiaries of said trust. The trusts' rules come down to the particular terms that apply to the given trust in question. Some jurisdictions allow for older members of the beneficiaries' class to ascend to the roles of trustee. Some of these jurisdictions actually allow for the grantor to be both a trustee and lifetime beneficiary together at once.

Two different types of trusts exist, the testamentary trust and the living trust. The testamentary trusts are also known as will trusts. These determine the means in which the assets for the individuals will be allocated after they eventually pass away. The document of such a trust comes into play legally following the death of the testator.

On the other hand, living trusts are known as inter vivos or revocable trusts. These written out documents allow for the assets of an individual to be created in the form of a trust. The individual himself or a beneficiary will then enjoy the advantages of and utilization of the resources throughout their remaining lives. Such assets will eventually be transferred to the legal beneficiaries when the individual dies. The trust creator sets a successor trustee who will carry the responsibility of transferring any remaining assets over to the beneficiary in question.

There are a number of different reasons that individuals employ trusts. One of these is to attain a degree of privacy. Wills and their arrangements are often public domain material in many jurisdictions. Trusts can specify the identical conditions which a will may, without the intrusive nature of being public domain documents available for any and all members of the public to read upon demand. This explains why those people who do not wish to have their wills and terms of their estate disposition revealed publically after they are gone will often choose to utilize trusts for their final bequests instead of the will document.

Besides this, trusts are a useful vehicle for planning the payment of taxes. Trusts have different tax arrangements than do standard planning accounts and competing vehicles. The tax consequences for deploying such trusts are typically less negative and expensive than those of other typical means involved in financial planning. This helps to explain why using trusts has become a standard option in the world of efficient tax planning. This is the case not only for individuals but also for corporations.

Finally, trusts find extensive utilization in estate planning procedures. This allows for the assets of deceased people to be passed on to their spouses. The spouses are then able to equally divide up the remaining assets for the benefit of the children who survive the deceased parent. Those children who do not possess the necessary 18 years of age to be considered legal persons (with possession rights) will be required to have trustees to exercise control over all assets in question until they reach the legal age of adulthood.

Trustee

Trustee refers to either a firm or an individual who possesses assets or real estate property on behalf of a third party individual, group, or organization. Trustees are often appointed to perform a great range of functions. These could be for charities, bankruptcies, trust funds, pension plans, or retirement plans.

As the name implies, these individuals or firms are entrusted with taking the optimal decisions which are in the primary interest of the beneficiary. Because of this sacred trust, these are often considered to be fiduciary responsibilities for the beneficiary or beneficiaries of the trust in question. This means that they are legally bound and obligated to perform these duties to the very best of their capabilities.

The granting of the prestigious title and responsibilities of trustee comes in the form of a legal title bestowed by a trust. Trusts themselves prove to be legal arrangements which two willingly consenting parties agree to make. Because of the fiduciary nature of the trustee role in any trust which the individual or organization oversees for the beneficiary or beneficiaries, they must lay aside any and all hopes of individual gain or personal agendas so that they can perform the best actions on behalf of the trust.

In other words, the trustee carries the full responsibility for correctly and optimally managing both the financial assets and real estate types of property which the trust itself possesses. There will always be duties particular to the specific details of the trust which the trustees must perform. The differing types of assets will naturally dictate the activities which the trustees must engage in for the beneficiaries' common good.

It helps to consider a real world example to more fully understand the somewhat complex concept. When trusts are made up of a range of real estate properties, the trustees will be responsible for properly overseeing the maintenance and handling of the particular pieces of property. In other cases, a trust might be comprised of different investments such as stocks, mutual funds, and bond holdings in a stock brokerage firm account. The trustees in this case will have to properly oversee and mange as necessary the account or accounts for the beneficiaries.

Trustees also have certain guidelines to which they must adhere in general. Among these common responsibilities which pertain no matter what the particulars of the trust agreement may actually be, the assets must be at all times kept under the direct control of the trustees so that they are securely accounted for each and every day. Trustees also must fully grasp the often unique terms of their particular trust, the responsibilities they are incurring by taking on the role, and the wishes of the applicable beneficiaries. Assets which may be invested must be considered productive so that they will benefit the beneficiary or beneficiaries in the future.

Besides this, the trustees have to both understand and properly interpret the trust arrangement so that they can effectively administer the assets' distribution to the correct parties and/or beneficiaries. This includes the duties of compiling all appropriate records for the trust. Among these there will be tax returns which they must file and pay and statements that they must produce and deliver to the beneficiaries. As such, the trustees will be expected to maintain regular communication with all beneficiaries so that they remain informed of the value of related accounts and any taxes which will become due.

In the end, all trustees have the distinction of being the ultimate decision makers regarding every trust-related matter. They must make such decisions according to the particular provisions contained within their unique trust arrangement and contract. It also means that if beneficiaries have questions regarding a decision which the trustee is preparing to take, that they must first obtain answers for these beneficiaries before they engage in the given decision.

Underwriting

Underwriting refers to a means of determining if a consumer is eligible or not for a particular kind of financial product. These products vary depending on the person's or business' requirements. They might include home mortgages, insurance coverage needs, business mortgages, lines of credit, or financing for venture start up projects. The bank or other financial institution undergoing the underwriting evaluation procedure will look into the odds of the business transaction successfully providing them with a profit in exchange for their offer of financial help.

As banks and insurance firms go through the underwriting process, two different things will occur. The first of these is showing an interest in the project that the borrower is proposing for finance. They demonstrate this by offering the financial aid that the customer is requesting. Next, with a bank or institution underwriting an insurance policy, residential or commercial mortgage, or venture, they are looking to make money on their investment one day in the future. They might either gather these profits at one time in the form of a lump sum at a future date or little by little in monthly payments. In these underwriting activities, compensation is expected, which is commonly paid via finance charges or other fees.

Underwriters contemplate more than simply the amount of risk that an applicant demonstrates. They also consider the potential risk that working with the new customer might bring to other customers of their company. In order to ensure that the bank or firm does not suffer too much harm to keep up with commitments made to already existing clients, they have developed underwriting standards.

Insurance companies heavily rely on underwriting in performing their business. Health insurance is one example of this. Health insurance providers seriously look into the past and present health of a person applying. Sometimes their underwriting will show that they need to exclude various pre-existing conditions for a certain amount of time when they insure the person. Other times, underwriting will reveal a medical history that demonstrates too much risk for the company. In this case, a health insurance company will refuse to provide the requested health insurance coverage. Their goal is to not insure individuals who they believe will need significant medical treatment over time, so that they can provide a solid financial backing for their existing clientele.

In business, underwriting is commonly employed to determine if new ventures should be given financing. An example of this might be a company that has created a new technology that it wishes to sell. These underwriters will consider how marketable the product appears, the applicant's marketing plan, the expense of creating and selling the new items, and also the odds of the company realizing profits on every piece that they sell. Sometimes, underwriters of these business ventures will express an interest in having shares of stock in the start up company as a portion of their payment for services. Other times, they will only require a set interest rate for the dollar amount invested.

Venture Capital

Venture capital refers to the process of investors purchasing a portion of a start up company. Firms or individuals that engage in this are called venture capitalists. They pour money into a firm that offers a high rate of growth but that also contains high risk. The typical venture capital investment time frame generally proves to be from five years up to seven years. Such investors anticipate getting a profit back on their investment through one of two ways. Either they hope to sell their stake in an Initial Public Offering to the public, or they hope to sell the company outright.

Investors who involve themselves in venture capital investments often wish to obtain a certain percentage of the company's ownership. They might also request being given one of the director's seats. This makes it easier for the investors to ask to be given their funds back either through insisting that the company be sold or reworking the deal that they made in the first place.

Venture capitalist investments are comprised of three different kinds. One of them is early stage financing that might be broken down into seed financing, first stage financing, or start up financing. Seed financing means that a tiny dollar amount of venture capital is paid to an inventor or other entrepreneur who wants to open a business. This might be employed to come up with a business plan, do market research, or bring on a good management team.

First stage financing is the type needed as companies look to boost their capital so that they can begin full scale operations. Start up financing instead is venture capital distributed to a business that exists for under a year. In this stage, a product will not be on the market already, or will only just have been put on the market for sale.

A second type of venture capital investments is known as expansion financing. Expansion financing is comprised of both bridge financing as well as second and third stage financing. Bridge financing refers to investments that only receive interest and are short term. They are mostly employed for company restructurings. They might also be utilized to cash out early investors.

Second stage financing proves to be investment money for the purpose of growing a company already up and running. While such a company may not yet demonstrate actual profits, it is producing and selling merchandise. It also possesses inventories and accounts that are expanding.

Third stage financing is investments that venture capitalists make in companies that have at least broken even on costs or are even starting to demonstrate profits. In this case, venture capital is employed to grow the business further. For example, third stage financing could be utilized to develop more or better products, or to purchase needed real estate.

Still a different popular version of venture capital investing is known as acquisition financing. In this type of venture capital, the investment goes into gaining a stake in or the entire ownership of a different company. Management could also choose to use this venture capital to buy out yet another business or product line, whatever its development stage proves to be. They might acquire either a public or a private company in this way.

Volatility

Volatility in investments has to do with the possibility of stocks or other investments undergoing a dramatic gain or loss in price and value in a certain amount of time. Investors consider the volatility of stocks and other investments when they decide to buy more shares of the asset, sell their current holdings, or to buy shares of a new offering. Whatever an investment's volatility proves to be, investors' goal should always be to make the highest return that they possibly can for the lowest chances of experiencing losses.

With stocks, a great concern is how stable the assets of a company are that underlie the stock itself. A sudden loss of confidence in a public company would also likely cause a sharp decline in the price. The stock price drop and accompanying volatility is actually created by the public's perception of something within the company, like changing leadership or a coming acquisition.

In fact the stock might come back in a relatively short time frame as the public decides that the company is stable after all. But such factors might be more troubling and enduring, causing the volatility of the stock to become too high. When such volatility persists, many investors will decide not to buy additional shares or even to sell off the ones that they hold.

The overall conditions of a market can also influence investment volatility. As the stock market all around shows higher signs of volatility, individual investments will likely suffer the same fate. This occurs as consumers become worried about the whole economy, or if political situations force investors to take more conservative trading positions. Should such impacts grow sufficiently significant, then even stable stocks can become lightly traded while investors sit on the sidelines to watch for the troubling issues to get resolved. In the meanwhile, the stocks and their underlying options might make dramatic rises and drops in price from higher volatility.

Volatility is a fact of life that investors have to be capable of handling. Still, some stocks and investments demonstrate higher degrees of volatility than do others. Investors can gain an insight into this amount of individual volatility that an investment might have thorough looking into its historical levels of price and accompanying volatility.

Using this data with projected trends in the economy and markets, investors can get a good picture of the amount of an individual investment's volatility to determine if they are comfortable with it before they invest in the offering.

Wire Transfer

A wire transfer is the quickest, safest, most reliable means of sending money within the United States, in other countries, or around the world. They are often essential in the more critical financial activities of life such as purchasing a house. The reason larger transactions occur in this form of payment is because the recipient can receive and verify the funds transfer the same day it is done, or as near to immediately as possible (besides Western Union and Money Gram, which cost substantially more to utilize).

A wire transfer actually represents a means to electronically transfer money from one party to another via a bank as intermediary. A traditional and typical wire transfer starts at a credit union or bank and electronically processes through either Fedwire or SWIFT networks. Another common name for such a wire transfer is a bank wire, which also encompasses the standard bank to bank transfers.

Ultimately the wire transfers have become so successful and utilized throughout the United States and rest of world simply because they are capable of moving even enormous sums of money to any destination bank in the world in only a day or two. If they are affected within the same country such as the United States then same day wires can be done. For an international transfer via wire transfer, it often requires another day or even two to complete.

Since the funds move rapidly through the financial system, recipients are not required to wait a material amount of time for the funds to become cleared. This means they can access and utilize the money without significant delays. No holds are typically placed on wire transfer monies. The safety issue means that merchants prefer the wire mechanism. This is because checks can bounce because of insufficient funds, while wires never do so. In other words, these are guaranteed funds.

There are some particular requirements that wire transfers need in order to be possible to transact. At least in the United States, both parties would require a functioning bank account in order for a bank to act as intermediary. Since thieves can not open a bank account too easily, nor bank anonymously in the United States, it is difficult for them to carry out scams using bank wires. This is because it leaves a paper trail which is easy for law enforcement officials to follow.

This does not mean that wire transfer scams are unknown entirely. It is possible for a person to be tricked into wiring money to a fraudster for a purchase or service they never receive. Examples of this are fake insurance policies or false retirement or investment products. Once the wire has cleared the recipients account, they can either withdraw the funds in person or wire it to an offshore overseas account.

By the time the victims realize that they have been scammed, the funds sent by wire will be long gone. They would no longer be recoverable by traditional U.S. law enforcement or even court order methods once they have been transferred offshore. Pulling money back after it has been dispatched via bank wire is extremely difficult in any case. This is true even if the funds remain in the recipient's bank account.

Wire transfer fees can be significant. In many parts of the United States, they run as high as $40 to dispatch a bank wire. Many banks charge upwards of $10 in order for a bank wire to be received into an account. The costs to send one are higher if the wire is funded by utilizing a credit card cash advance. Cash advance fees would then apply, as well as typically large interest rates, plus the wire transfer fee. This is why it is typically most financially sound to effect a bank wire directly from the sender's bank account.

Other Books in this Financial IQ Series

99 Financial Terms

Personal Finance Terms

Real Estate Terms

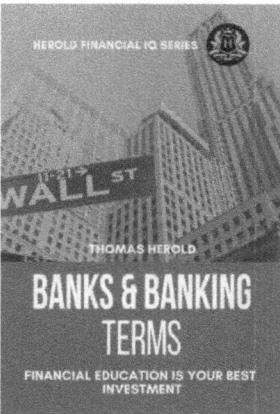

Banks & Banking Terms

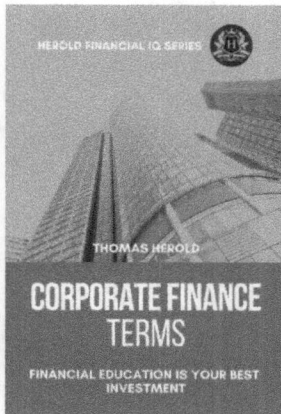

Corporate Finance Terms

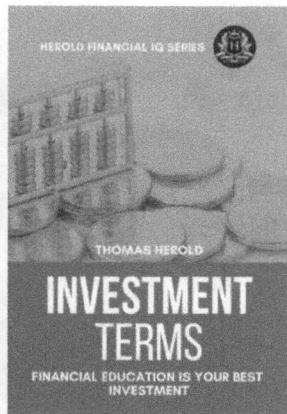

Investment Terms

Other Books in this Financial IQ Series

Economics Terms

Retirement Terms

Stock Trading Terms

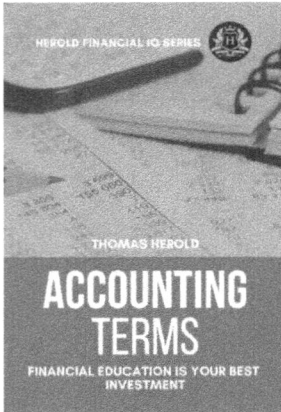

Accounting Terms

Debt & Bankruptcy

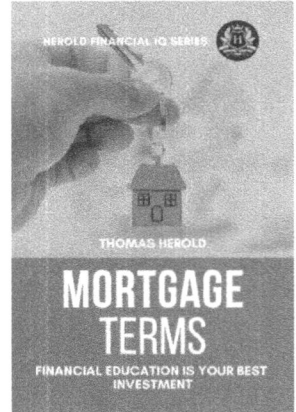

Mortgage Terms

Other Books in this Financial IQ Series

Small Business Terms

Wall Street Terms

Laws & Regulations

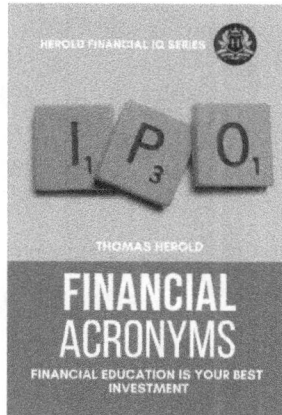

Financial Acronyms

www.ingramcontent.com/pod-product-compliance
Lightning Source LLC
Chambersburg PA
CBHW071600210326
41597CB00019B/3335